# Advance Praise for *Disrupters*

For the past 30 years, I have been building world-class diverse teams and engaging and developing women leaders. Dr. Patti's pragmatic approach to helping you become the CEO of your own career is sound and actionable advice that will lead to success in your personal and professional life.

—JOYCE BROCAGLIA, FOUNDER OF EXECUTIVE WOMEN'S FORUM

Readable, thoughtful, and wise, Dr. Patti Fletcher's *Disrupters* should be added to the business bookshelf of any woman or man who takes the challenges of diversity and inclusion to heart.

—TERESA NELSON, PH.D., FOUNDING PRINCIPAL OF THE IMPACT SEAT
AND PROFESSOR OF BUSINESS AT SIMMONS COLLEGE

Dr. Patti's book is your roadmap to live the life you want to live while achieving success as you define it on your own terms.

—BARBARA CLARKE, ANGEL INVESTOR, VENTURE CAPITALIST, AND
FOUNDING PRINCIPAL OF THE IMPACT SEAT

I've known Patti for many years, and her passion for helping women is impressive. She speaks from the heart, focuses on results, and uses her vast experience to bring meaningful advice to women who want to change the world.

—PENNY HERSCHER, FORMER TECH CEO AND PUBLIC COMPANY
BOARD DIRECTOR

In *Disrupters*, Dr. Patti distills experience, insight, and evidence to show how women win and why some "rules" are just guidance for other people. If you plan to change the world, drink deep within these pages.

—ROWAN GARDNER, CEO OF OZO INNOVATIONS LTD, UK

I write columns about entrepreneurship and crave intelligent insights. I can see I'll be using many quotes from *Disrupters*. There's a plethora of information in this book. Signs of a great read are: turned-down corners, underlined sentences, and scribbles in the margins. This is one of those books!
—EMMA SINCLAIR, MBE, CO-FOUNDER OF ENTERPRISEJUNGLE

Dr. Patti doesn't preach to the reader. She works with you to apply lessons learned from different women business leaders who have achieved success as they define it.
—SUSAN DUFFY, HEAD OF CWEL, BABSON

Pragmatic, direct, tough, insightful, passionate, and thoughtful. These words describe Dr. Patti Fletcher as much as her great new book. *Disrupters* is helpful for women from all walks of life, and it's no surprise someone as smart and talented as Patti has pulled it together in such a readable way.
—BOB FITTS, FOUNDER AND PRODUCER OF SUP-X: THE STARTUP EXPO AND SUP-X RADIO

As someone who's bonded with Patti over shared challenges, frustrations, and triumphs, I can tell you this is a business book for real business women. If you're like me, you'll find yourself nodding along or cursing under your breath. If you're tired of the ambiguous suggestions or utopian fantasies of other books, read *Disrupters*.
—BOBBIE CARLTON, FOUNDER OF INNOVATION WOMEN

I've dedicated my career to helping extraordinary women reach their full potential. I cannot stress enough the importance of the message and lessons from *Disrupters*—regardless of their age or where they are in their careers. Buy this book now for the women leaders in your life!
—JANE FINETTE, FOUNDER OF THE COACHING FELLOWSHIP

# disrupters

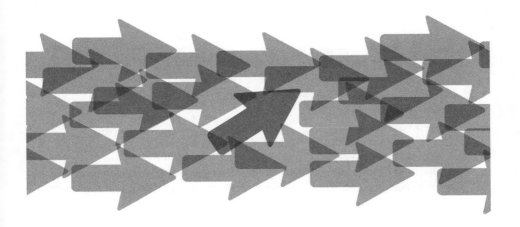

## SUCCESS STRATEGIES
## FROM WOMEN WHO
## BREAK THE MOLD

### DR. PATTI FLETCHER

Entrepreneur
PRESS

Entrepreneur Press, Publisher
Cover Design: Andrew Welyczko
Production and Composition: Eliot House Productions

This publication is designed to provide accurate and authoritative information
in regard to the subject matter covered. It is sold with the understanding that
the publisher is not engaged in rendering legal, accounting or other professional
services. If legal advice or other expert assistance is required, the services of a
competent professional person should be sought.

**Library of Congress Cataloging-in-Publication Data**
   Names: Fletcher, Patti, author.
   Title: Disrupters: success strategies from women who break the mold /
      by Dr. Patti Fletcher.
   Description: Irvine : Entrepreneur Media, Inc., [2018]
   Identifiers: LCCN 2017043525 | ISBN 978-1-59918-620-7 (alk. paper) |
      ISBN 1-59918-620-9 (alk. paper)
   Subjects: LCSH: Success in business. | Women—Vocational guidance.
   Classification: LCC HF5386 .F419 2018 | DDC 650.1082—dc23
   LC record available at https://lccn.loc.gov/2017043525

Printed in the United States of America

21  20  19  18                                    10 9 8 7 6 5 4 3 2 1

*For Nana, Mom, Almas, Dad, Geri, Karen, Chris, Heather, Mimi, Bella, Gabby, and Winnie*

# contents

**disrupters**

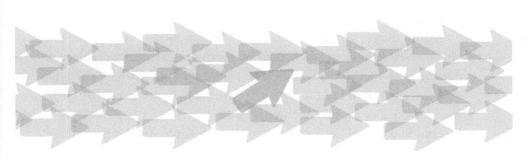

# foreword
# by Lisa Ling

I'm grateful for the opportunities I've had in my career. Despite not having a lot of resources growing up, I was fortunate to land a role in TV at just 16. Over the past 20-plus years, I've had the opportunity to work with National Geographic, OWN, ABC, and CNN. I've traveled the world and been able to do journalism the unique way I wanted to.

I always said that I would never use my gender to land any kind of concessions. To date, I've never felt that being a woman played a role in anything I've achieved. I've always felt that my work spoke for itself.

More than a decade ago, though, I had an incident that made me change how I think and feel about being a woman in the workplace. I got the news that my show would be picked up for a season. I thought that was great until I got the news that my male counterparts had their shows picked up for two or three seasons.

If it had simply been a matter of their shows having higher ratings than mine, I would have completely understood. That would have been a business decision. But they didn't. My show had ratings comparable to theirs, if not slightly higher in some cases. There was no justification for them not picking up my show for as many seasons as they did my white, male peers'.

For the first time in my life, I felt that my gender and ethnicity went against me. My work did speak for itself, yet it wasn't being recognized. My numbers were just as good, if not better, and yet their shows had secured multiple seasons versus my one.

Why?

Growing up as an Asian-American, my culture taught me not to rock the boat; don't do anything that would jeopardize your job. At the same time, my father raised me to not let my gender be an inhibition.

I also felt guilty about wanting to ask for more. In fact, my talent agents beg me, "Lisa, don't negotiate your contracts. Let us do it for you because, otherwise, you'll do it for free." And they're right! I love what I do so much that I would probably do it no matter how little the networks offered. I love my work.

So there I was, dealing with all of these conflicting emotions. One part of me felt angry that I was being passed over. Part of me chided myself for wanting to rock the boat; I should just be glad that I was even being picked up for a season and not worry about others being disproportionately rewarded. Then, of course, there was the guilt about not being appropriately grateful for what I had.

I didn't even have children at the time, but for some reason, I just imagined what advice I would give my daughter years from now if she found herself in my shoes.

There was no hesitation. I knew immediately what I would tell her: that she should stand up for herself and demand her worth. If she had done work comparable to others, then she should have comparable opportunity. I would want my daughter to fight for herself, just as I would my son.

In the years since that incident, I have had two daughters. I realize that standing up for myself *is* standing up for them. Just as my hero Connie Chung paved the way for Asian women like me in television, everything I do makes it easier for my daughters coming after me.

When I stand for myself, I'm standing for women everywhere.

I'm glad I did. When I met with the executives, I said, "I think it's very white and male of you to pick up these guys' shows for several seasons and mine for one. My ratings are commensurate, if not higher. I also think it's important for people to see a woman and an Asian hosting a show. I don't understand your justification for your decision."

They said, "You're right. Why wouldn't we pick up your show for as long as theirs?" And just as easy as that, I had an extra season.

They had no malicious intent. They had no hidden agenda. There was no explicit bias. I truly believe they just didn't see me the same way they saw others who looked like them. It's an example of what Patti talks about throughout this book: unconscious bias. When people who've been doing things a certain way for a long time, they're predisposed to keep doing them that way. The less diversified our places of work are, the less representation we see at the highest levels, and the less we have different kinds of people surrounding us, the harder it is to be sensitive to the needs of those outside our own personal spheres. It wasn't that the network executives had a bias against me so much as it was that they had a bias toward the way they'd always done things.

If I hadn't seen Connie Chung on the nightly news, I don't know that I would have tried to be a journalist myself. Seeing people who look like us in those positions is deeply important. To see women at the helm of Fortune 500 companies or as leaders in Congress lets other women know that they can achieve that, too.

When I gathered my courage and confronted those executives, I thought, *I'm doing this for all women—and especially for the generations who come after me.* But no matter what I do, no matter how hard I fight, no matter how much I advocate equity, it will never be enough. My show getting picked up for a season isn't going to change the status quo. I can't make a real difference on my own.

But *we* can.

When all of us stand up for ourselves . . . when all of us demand our worth . . . when all of us stop trying to be superwomen and just let ourselves be women . . . when all of us see ourselves as part of the bigger picture and realize how our collective efforts change the future for our daughters and granddaughters—that's when we'll begin to see true change.

This is what *Disrupters* is really about. On one level, it's practical: "here's what you can learn from different women who have achieved success." On a deeper level, it's mission-driven: "here's *why* you need to achieve success—not just for yourself, but for women everywhere."

I applaud Patti for taking this issue on now. I am so grateful for the opportunities I've had because of the people who paved the way before me. Now, it's my turn to do the same for those who come after me.

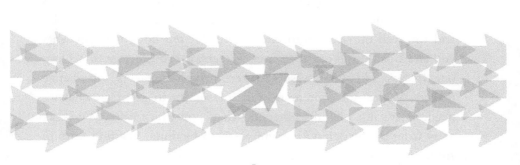

# introduction

*"You've come a long way, baby."*

—Virginia Slims ad

It hasn't even been a century since the U.S. passed the 19th amendment granting women's suffrage. One canton of Switzerland held out as recently as 1991. Saudi Arabia just allowed women to cast votes and run for office in 2015.

I am grateful for the progress we've made . . . but I am not satisfied.

You aren't satisfied, either. You picked up a book titled *Disrupters* because you want to see change. And as the Dalai Lama tweeted, "Change starts with us as individuals."

That's why this book is *not* about what companies and institutions can and should do to promote gender equity. We need those books, and we need our leaders to read them. But *this* book is about what you and I can do in our own lives, careers, and businesses to achieve our dreams. This book wasn't written for policy makers, but change makers. We're not content to wait for society to grant us what we need. That's not what disrupters do; that's not who we are. We break away from the way things are supposed to be done. We find ways to zig when everyone else zags.

If you're looking for a career book on how to succeed in a man's world, *Disrupters* isn't for you. If you're looking for a business book on finding success in the world by doing things your own way . . . well, this is a great place to start.

I can't promise you'll find the answers you need for the problems you face in these pages. I can promise you'll find inspiration. I can promise you'll have your eyes opened to the reality of the challenges you face. I can promise you'll find examples of women just like you who have faced hardships and found ways to overcome them. *Disrupters* isn't about me; it's about you. It's about equipping you with the knowledge, confidence, and maybe even that extra boost of courage you need to succeed. To do that, use the tools in this book. I've included stories (of success and failure alike) from women who forge their own paths. You'll also see a fair amount of research derived from my life's work of analyzing trends about women in business. The wonk in me knows that in order to make a point, you've got to show the evidence. I hope you'll find those numbers useful. Finally, this book includes plenty of tips and takeaways for how *you* can disrupt no matter where you are in the pecking order, from the warehouse floor to the C-suite.

Women are told—and we often tell ourselves—that we have all the opportunity we need. We have equal rights and equal access. Discrimination has been stamped out. Today, it's a level playing field. Whatever we do and don't achieve is on us. That's not entirely true. Then again, this book isn't about assigning blame. It's about finding practical solutions to the problems at hand.

The world is on the path to true gender equity. The problem is that it won't happen in our lifetime at the current rate. I have two daughters and will one day probably have granddaughters. What can I do in my sphere of influence to somehow move the needle faster? Perhaps you are asking yourself the same question.

As you might have gathered, this book has both an immediate goal and a long-term one. I want you to find your own path, as I and the women profiled throughout this book have. I want you to experience success *your* way.

As you find your success, though, you're blazing the path for my daughters and my granddaughters. Everything you do makes it that much easier for those who come after you. In finding your own success, you make it easier for those behind you to find theirs, too.

Let's go disrupt the world.

# know the game

*" . . . my real muse was David Bowie . . . He made me think there were no rules. But I was wrong. There are no rules—if you're a boy. There are rules if you're a girl . . . This was the first time I truly understood women do not have the same freedom as men."*

—MADONNA, ACCEPTING
BILLBOARD'S 2016 WOMAN OF THE YEAR AWARD

## HELP WANTED—IRISH NEED NOT APPLY

The Boston of my father's formative years was an era where that kind of blatant discrimination was not only acceptable but expected. Those signs hung in shop windows all over the city. To get a decent job during those times, the Irish had to hide their heritage to fit into a culture biased against them.

If he ever resented it, I never knew it. He just accepted that that's the way things were. Did he ever feel that it was wrong? That it was an injustice?

No, I don't believe he thought along those lines. He wasn't looking for social equity. And, to this day, I haven't seen my father describe himself as anything other than "American." For my father, being identified by a nationality beyond American was not as important as working hard by doing a day's labor for a day's pay, coming home, and quietly living his life.

If he could have changed things with just a wish, would he have wished for the roles to be reversed? For those of English heritage to be on the bottom rung of the social ladder and the Irish at the top? For the Irish to have more of everything: more privilege, more status, more importance?

That's not who my father was. He wouldn't have wanted anything special. He would have just wanted things to be fair. He would have wanted the rules that applied to him to apply to everyone else. Nothing less, nothing more.

That's all I want for women in business. I don't want special privileges. I don't want more freedom or more access than men. I just want equal freedom and equal access.

I'm not talking about whether a man opens a door for me. I love it when my husband treats me like a queen. I'm not talking about whether we refer to women on airplanes as "stewardesses" or "flight attendants." I don't care if you answer me with, "Yes, ma'am." That's not what really matters.

I am the first to say the way people lead and follow tends to be best defined by traits versus their anatomy, not all women lead like the women in this book, and not all men lead like the stereotypes and real-life examples in the pages that follow. Most of us have both female and male traits in how we present to the world. However, I cannot ignore the systematic problem that being a women who leads disruption presents in the world. I'm talking about the fact that women make up 50 percent of the Fortune 500 work force but hold only 4 percent of the CEO spots. I'm talking about when a man and a woman hold identical jobs, doing identical work producing identical results, and the woman still gets paid less. In the U.S., a woman gets paid anywhere from about 95 cents for every dollar a man works (according to 2009

## Going PC

I abhor the term "politically correct."

As a writer, I understand how powerful words are. I am glad that we are making an effort to take pejorative terms out of our collective vocabulary. We've begun using more gender-neutral terms: police officer instead of policeman; server in place of waitress. I can't remember the last time I heard someone say actress; today, they're all simply actors.

The problem with being politically correct is when you change your vocabulary without changing your underlying perspective. If we now refer to the woman at the front desk instead of the girl, it looks like we've made progress. But when we look at performance reviews, we see men being described as confident while women are aggressive; men are optimistic while women are naive.

It wouldn't matter if we changed every gender-laden word in every language: So long as people aren't seen as equals, it doesn't matter how polite you are when you refer to them.

report by the Department of Labor[1] and, more recently, a 2016 report "Demystifying the Gender Pay gap"[2]) to as low as 82 cents (per the 2012 study "Graduating to a Pay Gap: The Earnings of Woman and Men One Year after College Graduation[3]) . . . *for doing the exact same work.*

This figure is often quoted as 77 cents or 78 cents per dollar, but that number is somewhat misleading since it is the average pay gap between men and women. It does not account for occupation, position, education, seniority, hours worked, and other relevant factors as the other studies I just quoted do. More disheartening, the wage gap is even worse when you break out the various segments for women of color.

A good friend of mine who's a well-known expert in the tech field was challenged by her male colleague on the wage gap. He said, "Well, it's only a 5 percent difference in pay. I mean, we've basically solved the issue. The difference is immaterial."

She said, "Great, then I will have your 5 percent."

Perfect response. Point taken.

Worldwide, it's much worse than 5 percent, of course. The best estimate pegs the inequality at about 68 cents per dollar, according to a 2016 World Economic Forum Global Gender Gap Report.[4] I'm talking about not achieving true wage parity until 2099 (per that same report). Regardless of the study you review, all of them admit that there is a sizable piece of the gap that cannot be attributed to any sort of rationale—that, statistically, discrimination still exists throughout the world.

I'm talking about both the unconscious and explicit biases against women in business. How much more research do we actually need before change is made?

Like the Irish of my father's early childhood or others throughout history who occupied the lower rungs of the prevailing social order, most women probably shrug and say, "Well, that's just the way things are." Secretly we might want to be Joan of Arc or Susan B. Anthony and go change the world, but the rent notice quickly reminds us that we really need this job. We have to be practical. Really, what can any one of us do about it? Fighting for the right to vote or marching in Washington for the right to control our own bodies and our own destinies is one matter. Trying to win equality in the game of private commerce is a whole other animal.

Most of the research around gender equity concludes with governmental or corporate policy recommendations: gender quotas, promoting equal access, specific training, targeted recruiting, wage analyses, and so on. The overall message is, "Here's what you people at the top should do to help these women and minorities at the bottom."

It isn't working.

I've spent the past decade researching, coaching women business leaders, and advocating on our behalf. You know what I've learned about how successful women climb the corporate ladder to get past the glass ceiling?

They helped themselves.

*"If one man can destroy everything, why can't one girl change it?"*

—Malala Yousafzai

## Facing the Reality

In my doctoral research, I conducted a phenomenological study on 15 women trailblazers. I wanted to understand the key themes and common characteristics that defined their individual feelings, perspectives, and journeys, as opposed to performing a statistical analysis of hundreds of women. I could have studied women CEOs or senior-level executives, but I wanted insights into the most exclusive "boys' club" there was: boards of directors in life sciences and technology companies. At the time, these were some of the most male-dominated industries—and certainly the most technology intensive. My dissertation participants, all board members, were an impressive mix of corporate executives, entrepreneurs, and investors; many were or had been all three. If these women could reach that level of business success, where positions on a board of directors were almost exclusively filled by referrals from existing board members, surely they had something to share about how to navigate the world of business without losing themselves.

I took the findings from my research and compared it not only to my own experience but also to that of thousands of women I've worked with, led, managed, consulted for, advised, mentored, observed, and bonded with.

Here's the thing all of them have in common: Not one of them wakes up and says, "I wonder how I'll be oppressed today because I am a woman?" They don't see or think of themselves as victims.

They know there's a difference in how men and women are treated, of course, but until I start showing them the numbers—and telling them

# Word Power

Here are a few useful terms you should know as a disrupter:

**Bamboo ceiling**: The barriers keeping Asians from advancing higher up the corporate ladder (first coined by Jane Hyun)

**Career woman**: A woman who prioritizes professional achievements over her personal life

**Glass ceiling**: The invisible barrier keeping women (and especially women of color) from advancing higher up the corporate ladder

**Glass cliff**: When a woman is placed in a leadership role that has a high chance of failure

**Glass escalator/elevator**: When men are promoted faster than women in traditionally female-dominated roles

**Golden skirt**: A woman who sits on a disproportionately large number of boards of directors, e.g., Ann Mather at Alphabet, MGM, Netflix, and others; Delphine Arnault at LVMH, Fox, Ferrari, and Dior

**Mansplaining**: When a man explains something to a woman in a condescending or arrogant manner, usually while presuming to know more about the subject than she does (go Google "Rep. Pramila Jayapal mansplaining")

**Mommy track**: A career path of working women who are perceived to prioritize their home/personal life over their professional achievements after having children (as if they cannot accommodate both family and career)

**Second shift**: The additional unpaid work women do at home vis-à-vis their male partners

**Stained-glass ceiling**: The glass ceiling, but for religion

Sticky floor: The invisible impediment keeping women from being promoted as quickly as their male peers

Superwoman complex: The expectation placed on us (by ourselves, others, or society) to be great at being a mother, daughter, partner, worker, leader, housekeeper, volunteer, worshipper, cook, friend, sister, and anything else that pops up along the way

Third shift: In addition to the physical work of the first shift (working outside the home) and the second shift (taking care of the home afterward), women often work an additional shift: caring for their parents, philanthropic volunteering, and/or furthering their education

Work-at-home parent: A professional, often self-employed, who works from home to blend their professional and child-care responsibilities; for self-employed women, often referred to as a "mompreneur"

stories—they don't grasp the reality that industry culture, whether it's a large corporation or a startup ecosystem, is biased against women.

Sociology professor Christy Glass of Utah State said in 2013 that the awareness of gender inequality in business has faded out.[5] "I have my female students and they just don't think there's any lack of any opportunity for them in business," she said. "They don't think there's an issue. Then you show them some of the numbers."

You're probably much the same. You want to know how to win at work as a woman, but the first thing you have to do is realize the challenge you're up against.

You cannot win in the system if you don't know how it works.

## Fighting Second-Generation Gender Bias

It's no longer socially acceptable to openly discriminate against or sexually harass women (nor is it legal). We've moved past outright discrimination and made great strides toward equality. But the next frontier is what we call "second-generation gender bias": the subtle or even invisible barriers that continue to keep women from the upper echelons of business.

In the words of Dr. Glass, let's show you the numbers.

Women comprise almost half the U.S. work force, but how many of the S&P 500 have a female CEO? Twenty-six.[6] Twenty-six women out of five *hundred* chief execs.

This is how bad it is: If you're named John or David, you are four times more likely to be invited to sit on the board of a public company than *any* woman, according to S&P Global Market Intelligence's Compustat ExecuComp.[7]

The business world has had programs and initiatives for women since the 1970s, and women as a whole made strides up until the 1990s. Since then, though, the needle hasn't moved. We have more women in the global work force than ever before, yet there seems to be a quota for how many women are allowed to reach the top—a quota that hasn't changed in about two decades.

Don't buy the excuse that it's because most women work part time (nearly three-quarters work full time), or because they don't want to move higher up (mothers are more likely to have boardroom aspirations than female professionals without children—38 percent versus 24 percent, says McKinsey & Co.'s "Women in the Workplace 2015" report[8]). Don't believe it's because there's a lack of qualified candidates. There are plenty; you and I know some of their names.

According to the Jacquelyn and Gregory Zehner Foundation, a nonprofit focused on women's rights, women account for half of Ph.D.s, half of business school applicants, 67 percent of college graduates, and more than 70 percent of valedictorians across the U.S.[9]

*"Women and men are realizing that we need to move past the 1970s construction of women as a disadvantaged class. We need to move on to a 21st-century narrative through which women and men together create the kind of entrepreneurial class that best serves economic and social values."*

—Teresa Nelson

Despite that avalanche of talented, intelligent women, in the free-thinking, egalitarian, show-me-the-money world of venture capital, women-led companies received a paltry 2.19 percent of VC funding, per a 2016 data analysis by Pitchbook.[10] Men get a grossly disproportionate amount of all venture capital at 97.8 percent.

Why?

Is it because there aren't many startups founded and led by women? No. I sit on the board of Astia and am an investor with Astia Angels, vetting high-growth, women-led companies. We don't have a problem finding promising female entrepreneurs. Our challenge is figuring out which ones have more profit potential than the others. There are thousands of VC-worthy women out there. The fact that they receive only 2 percent of the pool of VC money points to a deeper issue than simply "there aren't enough women out there."

Furthermore, this isn't an American problem. It's global. To prove it, Figure 1.1 is a country-by-country breakdown, limited, of course, to the data available (I couldn't find trustworthy data from emerging economies):

*Figure 1.1* Deloitte Global's 2016 "Women in the Boardroom: A Global Perspective"[11]

| Country | Women, as Percentage of Work Force | Women, as Percentage of Total Board Seats |
| --- | --- | --- |
| Germany | 46% | 21% |
| U.K. | 46% | 22% |
| Australia | 46% | 20% |
| Spain | 46% | 16% |
| U.S. | 46% | 23% |
| Norway | 47% | 46% |
| France | 47% | 34% |
| Finland | 48% | 29% |

During South African apartheid, it was easy to see the discrimination from the numbers. Despite the country being only about one-fifth white, virtually every CEO, director, and executive were white. To mirror our data above, the numbers would look something like:

| Country | Whites, as Percentage of Population | Whites, as Percentage of Total Board Seats |
|---|---|---|
| South Africa | 19% | ~100% |

Of course it looks wrong: It was blatant discrimination. When one group of people—be it by ethnicity, gender, or other trait—is disproportionately underrepresented at the top, it signals a problem. In this case, it was a systemic bias against nonwhites.

Whenever we see that women represent nearly half the work force in some countries yet make up a quarter or less of the people at the top, it's a clear signal that something is wrong. In this case, it's a systemic bias against women.

*"Because I am a woman, I must make unusual efforts to succeed. If I fail, no one will say, 'She doesn't have what it takes.' They will say, 'Women don't have what it takes.' "*

—Clare Boothe Luce

## Yes, It's Happened to You

If you're a woman who's been employed more than five minutes, you've experienced the bias we're discussing here. Let me show you exactly what it looks like in real life.

One time, I was flying out of San Francisco. I found my aisle seat, settled in, and struck up a conversation with the guy in the window seat. It turned out that he was a business consultant, but one with a sense of humor. He launched into a hilarious tale about having to close down a winery, not being able to move the wine (I can't remember why), and going on a drinking binge of all this fine wine with his customers to celebrate a glorious business failure. I was cracking up two minutes into it.

We both crossed our fingers, hoping the seat between us would stay empty so we could continue our antics. No such luck.

Down the aisle came this stunning woman in her 50s or 60s. Beautiful Chanel suit, flawless makeup, coiffed hair—she was put together perfectly. She put her Prada bag in the overhead and then sat down in the middle seat. Since wine guy and I had already broken the ice, I thought it only polite to invite her to join in. From her bearing, I didn't think she would, but you never know.

It turns out she worked for a global IT company that I'd had some previous dealings with in my career. That led to me talking about the work I did supporting and coaching female executives in the IT space to overcome the systemic bias in corporate culture.

"You know, I've never experienced any of that. I guess I'm just lucky," Ms. Chanel Suit sniffed.

*OK*, I said silently. *Challenge accepted.* Not because I wanted to prove a point. If she was the rarest form of female executive—a highly qualified woman leader over 45 whose career has never been stunted because of her gender and age—then fabulous. I wanted to cheer her on. But if she wasn't, I wanted to bring the reality of the situation to her attention. I normally do not try to convert the unconverted. I focus on enabling leaders who want to change the world and are self-aware enough to know at least some of the barriers facing them, but there was something in the tone of her answer. (I also remember that my TV wasn't working and I needed something to pass the time.)

I said, "I guess you are," and then started asking innocuous questions about projects she had spearheaded.

She told me about this amazing initiative she had thought of, found support for, procured resources for, and poured hours into. In just a few minutes, though, she had a scowl on her face as she relayed the rest of the story: Once the project showed some promise, her boss—a young white dude—took over the project and presented it to his boss . . . also a young white dude.

Just earlier that week, the executive vice president, a woman, had presented the project to the entire division. The young white guys got the applause. No mention of Ms. Chanel Suit. No credit. No recognition of her initiative, her work, or her contribution. The two guys didn't invite her into the later meetings. Furthermore, they never gave her any support elsewhere and provided zero advocacy going forward.

As innocently as I could, I asked, "And does your boss do that to everybody?"

She thought for a moment and said, "No, he usually gives his support to the . . . oh. *Oh.*"

As soon as she realized that he always propped up the guys in his division—especially the young white dudes—and didn't give much support, if any, to the handful of women, she suddenly realized she *had* experienced this systemic bias.

She was transformed. Ms. Chanel Suit turned into an angry goddess on a mission to take control of her professional destiny. If

## Gender Equality vs. Gender Equity

"Equality" is the absence of negative action where all are treated the same; it assumes everyone has the same starting line, finish line, and journey.

"Equity" is the presence of positive action where each person is met where they are, not where you expect them to be.

Equality is not *dis*allowing a person of color to enroll in a university; equity is recognizing that a first-generation college student has a steeper set of challenges than someone who comes from generations of doctors and thereby creating a minority scholarship to mitigate that disadvantage.

Equity is not explicitly barring a woman from becoming CEO, yet continuing to say, "I just can't find any women candidates"; equity is recognizing that your candidate pool may be limited and thereby actively seeking out female candidates to balance it out.

awareness is the first step in the journey to recognizing bias, anger is usually the second. She started ticking off all the times that something similar had happened to her and other women, and all the times it didn't happen with her male co-workers.

"I'm going to call that EVP and tell her that it started with me," she said. "What do you think about that!"

It was too late, I told her. The idea had already been announced. Those two guys were recognized as the owners. If she tried to get the admittedly deserved credit for it, she'd look like a bitter old lady. The best route would be to congratulate them, be happy the idea took off, and start talking about the next new thing. Then she had to make sure it never happened again.

She's like so many of us, though. She had never stopped to question it. It was just something that happened. As a woman, you deal with it and move on. But once you start to look for it, you see it everywhere. This type of thing has been happening in the workplace every day, for at least a hundred years.

## A Century of Assimilation

Yes, plenty of men's ideas get stolen. Sometimes they're even stolen by women. This isn't men vs. women; us vs. them. It's not that black and white.

Her boss may not even realize he has an unconscious bias against the few women he manages. He has been conditioned in a system that was meant for our grandfathers, not for today's women.

The bias that women in leadership face isn't part of just one company or even of one culture. It's inherent, so deep-rooted that it's invisible. It's like asking a white person, "Hey, what's it like having white privilege?" You can't see it unless you're on the outside. And you can't see it, usually, unless you experience it firsthand and see it for what it is.

> **"Just because everything is different doesn't mean anything has changed."**
>
> —Irene Peter

It's been there ever since modern companies came into being. More than a century ago, Henry Ford's car factory in Highland Park, Michigan, started production. The Ford Motor Company hired so many employees who were newly immigrated to the U.S. that it created the Ford English School. It didn't just teach language skills and civics lessons. At its core, it attempted to transform immigrants into model citizens.

As Ford himself said of the school, "These men of many nations must be taught American ways, the English language, and the right way to live."

At the center of its graduation ceremony was a literal "melting pot." Graduates would enter the huge cauldron on one side decked out in native costumes representing their ethnicity: Someone born in Poland, for example, would look unmistakably Polish. After passing through the melting pot, their national identity would be boiled away. They would step out on the other side dressed identically in typical American clothes: dark suit, white shirt, and nice tie, replete with a boater hat, while smiling and waving American flags.

The Ford Motor Company had no room nor any use for diversity. Their assembly lines ran on mechanization, systemization, and uniformity. Henry Ford needed a worker who was replaceable and interchangeable. Having a dozen different languages and cultural norms on the factory floor got in the way of productivity.

You and I can look back and see how awful that was. We've learned to celebrate diversity. Trying to strip someone of their ethnic and cultural heritage is morally offensive to us. We have entire seminars today on being culturally sensitive. I can't imagine hearing someone saying, "You know, you'd really succeed in this company if you were just more American," much less a company hosting assimilation classes. Yet corporate culture still acts this way with women.

To succeed in a company, corporate culture expects women to shed what makes them unique—to be less like a woman and more like a man. If there are too few women in the higher echelons, the company blames the women: There are not enough qualified candidates, women don't want to move up, women lag behind their male counterparts

## Group Affinity

A 2015 report found that about twice as many men got help from senior-level men than did their female peers. It's an unconscious bias, not an explicit one. This is an "I" group affinity—i.e., a simple preference to be around "people like us."[12]

because they choose to have children, or whatever other excuse they can find.

In so many words, they're saying, "There's no room here for leaders who don't want to look and act like us. If only you acted more like a man, you could succeed."

No one says this, of course. I doubt many directors or CEOs even explicitly think it. It's an unconscious bias, which makes it even more difficult to combat. It's a cultural norm so embedded in corporate practice that it's a blind spot.

There are two main problems with this: One, we don't live in the Industrial Age anymore, and two, even women who assimilate still aren't guaranteed success.

We live in an economy where the chief competitive advantage doesn't come from mass-producing something more cheaply than your competitors. Margins and commodities are important, of course, but that's not a sustainable competitive advantage. The global economy is largely driven by innovation. And that doesn't come from group-think or uniformity, but from a mash-up of ideas and cross-collaboration. Assimilating everyone into the collective hive is the opposite of fostering innovation.

But look at some of the women you know who have assimilated. They may dress like men, negotiate like men, communicate like men, and mimic men in so many other little ways. Even so, ask yourself: Have they advanced as quickly as the male co-workers they started with? Have younger, less-qualified guys been promoted over them?

In any given scenario, would the same thing have happened to them if they had been men? If they were men . . . would they be where they are in their career right now?

## The Economic Cost of Gender Bias

To quote startup investor Adam Quinton of Lucas Point Ventures, speaking at the 2013 We Own It Summit, "It goes beyond fairness. This is a people's issue, not just a women's issue. As someone once said, 'It's the economy, stupid.'"

Another investor at that same summit, Richard Nunneley, put it this way: "Why waste 50 percent of global intellect?"

To round this out with a third sentiment, intellectual property lawyer Annette Kahler wrote in a 2011 paper examining the gender gap in patents, "Opportunities are being missed because the ideas, inventions, perspectives, and proposed solutions of women are missed."[13]

McKinsey Global Institute undertook a study in 2015[14] that examined gender inequality in 95 countries. Essentially, the authors posed the question, "What would it look like if women were as much a part of the economy as men?" If that were to happen, their research suggests, women would add $28 trillion to the global economy by 2025. To put that in perspective, they point out that this is roughly the size of the U.S. and Chinese economies *combined*. Can you imagine?

**"***Gender equality is smart economics.***"**

—Robert Zoellick, president of
the World Bank, 2007–2012

Of course, total gender parity is unlikely by 2025. To set more realistic expectations, they measured what the global economy would look like if each country just matched the progress of gender equality of its fastest-improving regional neighbor (out of ten groupings of regional countries)—in other words, if every country kept up with whoever was setting the pace toward economic parity in the region.

In that scenario, it was still an astounding $12 trillion.

# U.S. Businesses Majority-Owned by Women

Total number: +11 million

Percentage of all U.S. businesses: 38 percent

Gross revenue: +$1.6 trillion

Employing: 9 million people

Businesses with +$1 million in revenue owned by a woman: 1 in 5

#1 state by total number: California

#1 state by percentage: Louisiana

#1 state for fastest growth of number: Florida

Number by a woman of color: 5 million

*Sources*: National Women's Business Council Analysis of 2012 Survey of Business Owners; National Association of Women Business Owners Institute for Entrepreneurial Development; American Express OPEN 2016 State of Women-Owned Businesses Report[15]

That's how much women currently in the work force would add to the global economy today if they were paid equally to their male counterparts. That's an entire extra China churning out products and services . . . sitting right here in our collective backyards.

How do they suggest accomplishing this? Nothing earth-shattering. Their recommendations are along the lines of top-down approaches you see elsewhere: address unpaid labor and care, reduce violence toward women, ensure they have legal rights and protections, provide better education and access to health care, and so on.

Women everywhere need those things. Every woman should have the same rights and access as men. What's frustrating is that the conversation on gender still revolves around justifying why a woman should be in the room.

Why? Why do we have to prove that we can contribute just like our male counterparts? Why is the focus on "Yes, you have the right to be here" instead of "What do we need to make our board and company the most successful they can be?"

*That* should be the discussion. We shouldn't still need to do research on what the world would look like if women were accorded the same respect as men. Women and minorities shouldn't need to prove that we're capable. We should already have moved past those arguments. Indeed, we've made tremendous strides from the days when women couldn't even own property or vote. But our competence is not assumed. Our worth isn't recognized. Our rights aren't universal.

It does frustrate me. It does, at times, anger me. There is a systemic bias against women in corporate culture. You're not fighting any one person or even a group of people; you're fighting against a cultural mindset. But getting mad will only make it worse. You and I could drink Prosecco all night, ranting and railing against the Man, and solve nothing. And truly, that's not productive for the soul, either.

But what about the women who have made it to the top? What about the women who didn't assimilate? For my doctoral dissertation, I studied women who had not just broken the glass ceiling but shattered it. I could have done my research on successful female vice presidents and CEOs, but I wanted to go to the tip-top: women sitting on the boards of public companies in the highly competitive fields of technology and health care.

I wanted to understand their common traits and characteristics. What worked for them? What didn't? Did they attribute their success to luck or skill or knowing the right people? What did these women do differently than their peers that let them reach the pinnacle of corporate success? More important, could other women model it?

# The Way of the Disrupter

After concluding my research, I took my findings out into the real world. I compared notes with other accomplished female leaders at all levels, I coached female executives to success, I sat on the boards of organizations providing support and angel investment for women-led companies, and I implemented my findings in my own life and career.

With the odds stacked against them . . . when playing a rigged game . . . when working in a culture where unconscious bias against them is normal . . . how do women disrupters still achieve success? I've organized the rest of the book around what you need to know to break the mold and find your success.

## Know the Game

Here in Chapter 1, we've focused on the fact that, first and foremost, disrupters realize that business is a game, albeit one like Calvinball in "Calvin and Hobbes": You don't necessarily know what the rules are and often lose without even knowing why. But also like Calvinball, each player gets to make up her own rules.

So they do.

Later, you're going to read about Jo-Ann's portfolio approach to ever-changing business situations and how Nicole shook up an entire industry by redefining how high-growth startups are supposed to work.

## Define Your Own Success

Disrupters don't look to external sources to tell them what success looks like for them. They know that every individual has her own finish line. Some women want to embody Mother Earth, while others want to be the next Margaret Thatcher. Disrupters have a deep sense of their life's purpose, and nearly everything they do aligns with that vision.

Look for that theme while you read the profile of the venture capital investor who was shunned by her entire professional network as she pursued what she thought was best for the world.

## Choose Career *and* Family

They don't buy into the myth that you can be successful at home or successful at the office—but not both. These women find a way to achieve not work-life balance (there's no such thing) but work-life integration. They don't allow others to set their priorities or tell them how their life is supposed to look. They eschew what they're "supposed to do" and instead create their own goals and definitions of success. They find ways to weave the different strands of their lives together into a harmonious whole.

In Chapter 3, I'm going to share what that looks like for my husband and me, for other women, and even for a VC-funded entrepreneur whose husband is *also* a VC-funded entrepreneur. That blend of career and family looks different for all of us, but our approaches work for us.

## *Get Out of Your Head*

The first person to stop us is, unfortunately, ourselves. Before we can talk about how we can work around an external unconscious bias, we need to look at our own internal biases holding us back. The disrupters I present throughout this book have learned how to overcome their own self-doubt and fears. They still experience them, of course, but they know how to quiet and even ignore that voice inside their head.

Women's leadership styles often evoke resistance, exasperation, and even ridicule from their male co-workers, superiors, and subordinates. Women "don't make decisions fast enough" or "worry too much about people's feelings." Disrupters, however, have an enduring belief that they have the skills and capabilities to meet the challenges ahead. Or, if they don't, that they have the capacity to master the required skills. In other words, these women believe they have what it takes to lead—and so they do. Following this chapter, you're going to read about Lisa Morales-Hellebo's journey in "A Fully Formed Woman—Finally!" I see the journey of every disrupter mirrored in some aspect of her story.

disrupters

## Use What You've Got (Everyone Else Does)

Disrupters know the game is rigged and use every advantage they have to combat those odds. At the same time, they know that being a woman in business carries some unique risks, from being accused of landing a job "just because" they're a woman to the "glass cliff" phenomenon.

## Take the Damn Job!

Women are more likely than men to feel unprepared for a new position or set of responsibilities. We often rely on our demonstrated competence to judge whether we are prepared. Men, however, more often rely on confidence in their abilities. That is, we want to figure it out first and then take the job, while men want to take the job and then figure it out as they go.

This chapter consists of a short list of strategies disrupters use to advance their careers, followed by the profile of an unorthodox career path, which began in a drug rehab facility and wound up presenting in a United Nations compound.

## Mentoring Works! (Except When It Doesn't)

Many companies, some of them well-meaning, have created mentoring programs wherein they assign junior female employees to be coached by their more senior counterparts. These work well early in a woman's career, as young professionals come onboard and learn about the organization and how business works. But they don't affect how many women are later promoted to higher positions: women face the same glass ceiling regardless of whether they go through mentoring.

The more cost-effective approach would be to make upper management go through diversity training. Instead of trying to make women fit into the corporate mold (à la Henry Ford), why not make upper management change? Why not train them to be more inclusive and accommodate diversity in a way that would leverage talents and opposing perspectives to the benefit of their business? Teach them to incorporate those differences in a way that would make their company

one | know the game ✒ 21

more competitive, more innovative, and more like the customers they're trying to attract?

Disrupters actively seek mentoring—they just ensure it's the right kind. This chapter is about understanding the different types of support that may be available and how to use that support to achieve your vision of success. Following this discussion on mentoring programs and other diversity initiatives, we'll take a look at Dr. Gabriela Burlacu's work on the ways technology can advance these efforts.

## Thrive in the Tribe

I hate networking. You hate networking. Every woman I know hates networking. That's why disrupters don't do it. Instead, they create "tribes" of their like-minded, like-spirited peers. Leaders inside and outside my dissertation group told me that creating and maintaining a strong network of like-minded women was a key element of their success.

These support groups go beyond just chatting over coffee. These are strong, mutually reinforcing, formal and informal networks wherein women advise each other, offer professional perspectives, critique ideas, and—perhaps most important—connect friends and colleagues. I myself was invited into a tribe co-led by Miriam Christof, whose profile goes in-depth on the process of creating a thriving tribe of sisterhood.

## Lead Like a Woman

There are physiological differences between men and women. I don't think anyone would dispute that fact. We do think differently. We do engage in our workplaces differently. Instead of subsuming their natural approach to leadership, disrupters celebrate the differences. Chapter 9 focuses on the contrast between the ways men and women usually lead, but let me stress a critical takeaway upfront: A great company needs both.

In fact, this "androgynous" approach to leadership is one of the reasons Globalization Partners has succeeded as a high-growth company. Not only do I share the company's success story in this chapter, but I also do a deep dive in the accompanying profile of the founder and CEO, Nicole Sahin.

## Open the Door for Someone Else

Finally, disrupters always look to pay it forward. When the women I've observed, studied, and worked with reach a new position, they immediately begin trying to pull other women up with them. They become advocates and champions of their talented peers, advancing the cause of women in leadership roles. They don't worry about the potential competition or being seen as the resident bra-burning women's libber. They simply want other deserving women to be given the same opportunities that men have and to move their organization further down the road toward gender equity.

As you'll see, the research shows that greater diversity leads to greater financial performance, both in the short term and over the long haul. Gender equity is an organizational as well as an economic imperative. We need more gender diversity in leadership at all levels. To that end, we wrap up the book with a profile of Pat Milligan, a woman on the Global Agenda Council for the World Economic Forum in Davos.

It doesn't matter if you want to homeschool your children, build a business empire, run for city council, or weave some beautiful blend of all those: The world needs what you have to offer.

We need you to lead.

## Open the Door for Someone Else

# tech vs. the psychology of bias

B renda Reid is the vice president of product management at SAP SuccessFactors and currently focused on enabling businesses to leverage technology for onboarding as well as for diversity and inclusion strategies across the enterprise.

She is everything a tech company wants and more in a software product executive, placing the customer at the center of every decision. Using a healthy mix of empathy, pragmatism, and grit, Brenda has overseen aggressive product road-map development in one of the most competitive markets in the industry. While her professional achievements are remarkable, what has made the biggest impression on me is Brenda's trajectory.

We all have a story. Hers is that she was a teenage mom. With the support of her family, she finished school, earned her degree, and built a career in technology—one of the more unfriendly work forces for women, and especially working moms. Knowing how fortunate she was to have the support of her family, she spends her free time working with teen moms to give them a shot at achieving their goals and ambitions.

**Brenda, let's jump right in: Talk about your work with human resources technology. How does it move diversity and inclusion into the norm of HR strategy and planning?**

We tend to look at diversity through the rearview mirror: "We have X number of people in this role," or "We have this many candidates in our mentoring program," or "We had a hundred people in our diversity workshop." We count heads.

The questions around diversity tend to be reactive: "We don't have enough diversity in this department. How do we get more representation?" "We aren't hiring enough diversity candidates—how do we fix that?" Diversity is often seen as a problem to be solved, rather than an opportunity to be taken advantage of.

Measurement is important, but it doesn't change the path forward. When I began digging into the challenges of diversity and inclusion, my thought was that we needed to get out in front of bias. Forced trainings aren't the way to accomplish that. They're important, but they may only truly change the way one in maybe a thousand people go about their business. For the most part, people participate in diversity initiatives because they have to.

The research shows that most people do believe that diversity and inclusion are important. They do want to see their diversity hires and minority colleagues succeed in the company. The bias that exists is not an explicit one, but an unconscious bias. That's why training has limited effectiveness: It addresses the conscious part of how we make decisions, but it can't really help with our unconscious decisions.

That's why I'm so passionate about what tech can do to detect and eliminate bias: We can leverage technology to interrupt decision making at every point along a person's career journey.

Think of yourself as a manager, for example. There are all these different decision points when it comes to evaluating the performance of your team. You decide who to give raises to, what performance scores to give people, how to allocate bonuses, when and why to promote someone, how you go about developing someone, what opportunities to present to them—these are all points where your unconscious decision making comes into play. When people make decisions that consistently favor one demographic over another, 90 percent of the time it's not because of malicious intent. It's just because of making decisions quickly, whereupon we heavily rely on the unconscious parts of our brain.

When you're about to make one of those decisions, technology can interrupt a potentially biased determination. Often, it just takes asking an explicit question to make someone reconsider and potentially have them go down a different path.

There was a study once on interrupting decision making around cyberbullying. They carried out a test on a group of teenagers wherein the software would detect certain words and phrases that were flagged as inflammatory or insulting. When the teenager hit "post," a message box popped up that said something like, "It looks like you're about to post something that could be harmful or bullying to someone. Are you sure you want to continue?"

Ninety percent of the time, they changed their mind. Just taking that extra moment to consider "Do I really want to post this?" prompted teenagers to make a different decision about how their actions would affect someone else.

In the workplace, I'm sure you wouldn't see that kind of percentage, but the mere act of bringing a potentially biased decision to someone's attention can result in different outcomes.

*What would the "act of bringing a potentially biased decision to someone's attention" look like? A pop-up box that says something like, "It looks like you're about to make a biased decision, you low-down misogynist"?*

Say you're sitting down to do the dreaded performance review. Everybody hates doing performance reviews, so you rush through them as quickly as possible. In doing so, you're often making rushed judgments. For example, in the HR world, you're not allowed to penalize someone for a leave of absence, right? You're not supposed to let that influence your performance review of anyone. So if you were to score someone comparatively low, you might have a message pop up that says, "I see you're about to rate this person lower than you did last year. I also noticed that they took a leave of absence earlier this year. Is it possible that that's influencing your score?"

It could bring up a set of maybe four objective criteria to ensure that you're rating her fairly, instead of by a set of subjective measures. Just asking the question might make you say, "You know, I am irritated with her because she didn't get that project finished . . . but that was really because she took some family leave. When she got back, though, her productivity was excellent. I really shouldn't punish her for that."

Just interrupting a manager's decision-making process to make them think about something a little more deeply can result in a different score. It's just explicitly asking, "What's influencing this decision of yours? Are you sure this is the decision you want to make?"

A different score on a performance review can alter the trajectory of a person's career. Those metrics affect who's targeted for promotion, who's seen as a potential rising star, how their raises and bonuses are calculated, and how they rank against their peers. Those decisions affect a person's career direction, which is potentially life-altering. You've changed their future.

Take this true example: A group of managers was doing performance reviews for the team members for whom they shared supervisory responsibility. One of the criteria was on organizational potential. When the group got to one team member, one manager was surprised that another manager had rated this team member—let's call her Sally—fairly low. In the manager's experience, Sally was smart and incredibly capable.

She asked her fellow manager, "I'm just curious: Why did you rate Sally so low on potential?"

He said, "Well, I know she just had a baby and that she is really struggling with just wanting to stay home. I mean, my wife just had a baby, too, and I know how overwhelmed she is. If I scored Sally higher, it would get her into high-potential programs, and I know she just doesn't want that right now."

Here was a man who truly had nothing but the very best of intentions for Sally—he was just going about it the wrong way. In that instance, if the technology had been in place around that one criterion, it could have asked, "Have you had a conversation with this person about their career aspirations?"

Even in a case where someone's organizational potential was low, if that team member had indicated a desire to advance in the company, then the system could send up a red flag that there was an issue between the employee's expectations and her supervisor's assessment.

The point, though, is that these micro-actions can impact an employee. These types of tiny course corrections along the way can change someone's whole trajectory.

*We say we want to eliminate bias, but that's a lofty goal that involves identity, societal norms, and a lot of factors technology can't touch. However, tech like this could at least mitigate that bias.*

Exactly. If you can make someone aware of an unconscious bias, not only can you help them avoid it, but over time they begin asking themselves those questions. It changes their thinking pattern and their internal decision tree. We're never going to eliminate bias, but we can make it less prevalent.

Let's say you're a manager for ten people, and bias detection software helps you make a slightly different decision for the three women. Maybe the software detects that you consistently rate women lower in a couple of areas—showing initiative, for example. Or it may not be that you rate women lower but that you consistently rate aggressive men higher. If the software makes you pause to consider whether those women truly display less initiative, or it just looks different coming from them, then that's three women for whom the tech has made a difference. The cumulative effect would change the makeup of the people up for promotions and potentially stem the leaky talent pipeline. You would have made enormous strides toward gender equity in your company.

This isn't a forced diversity and inclusion training, it isn't a big HR initiative, it's not some expensive mandatory program—it's just the simple act of helping someone bring an unconscious decision over to the conscious side of their mind and letting them quickly re-examine their thinking to ensure it's their best decision.

***So performance reviews are one area where tech could mitigate bias. What's another?***

Tech could support specific diversity and inclusion targets. Say, for instance, your company set an explicit goal to hire X percent more women this year. The problem with such a policy is that there's no process for implementing it. Without it, while hiring X percent more women may be the company goal, the people doing the recruiting and hiring are still relying on their own judgment to recruit and hire—which means relying on a lot of unconscious decision making.

With software, you could say, "We want to hire X percent more women this year, and we're going to enforce that at the interview stage: At least half the candidates being interviewed must be women." You can then use the applicant tracking system—which nearly every big company already uses today—to enforce that quota: Half of all people interviewed must be women.

This goes back to my point about getting in front of the bias rather than going through the recruiting and interviewing stages and then saying, "Hey, we haven't met our diversity goal this year. What happened?"

*As we've discussed before, the research says that unconscious gender bias isn't limited to just men.*

No, not at all. In my experience, I've seen women who are more biased against other women than they are men. Those guilty of unconscious bias can be from any gender and any background.

On the other hand, those of us who do actively advocate gender equity can sometimes open the door a little too far. I once had a woman on my team ask me if I was trying to get rid of her. I said, "Oh, dear God, no! I love working with you! Why would you think I wanted to get rid of you?"

She said, "Because you keep presenting me with all these opportunities to do other things and encouraging me to take advantage of them. I felt like you were trying to get me to go elsewhere."

We had a good relationship, so we could later laugh about it, but it was a real eye-opening moment for me. As women, we do try to lift up other women, but I had done so to a fault!

*Yet as we both know, technology is only one piece of change.*

The first consideration is: Is the work force even ready?

Technology is an enabler. It can't eliminate bias; it can only detect it and help make you aware of it. But the driver of change has to be the culture of the organization itself. Are the people in your company ready to accept these kinds of changes? Do they "get" diversity and inclusion?

This is especially true around the people configuring the technology. Do they buy into the concept and need for gender equity? If they don't, the software can't fix that.

Take one of your pet peeves, Patti: mentoring programs. You and I have seen them done right and become a real asset for women—but only when the people setting up the program really understand the purpose of mentoring and what a successful outcome looks like. For mentor programs like that, technology can be a great enabler because it's going to be configured right in the first place. It can help sort and filter the right participants with the right mentors; it could enable people who want to be mentors but don't know how to effectively connect with potential mentees.

An even bigger cultural consideration is: How risk-averse is your company? It's sad to say, but many big companies don't want to crack the door on this issue. They'd rather turn a blind eye and not know than open the data and see just how ugly it is. Ignorance is bliss, right?

If that's the culture of your workplace, then you have to be careful as a gender-equity advocate. You need to gauge how open your leadership is and who could be your potential ally (or accomplice!) in advancing diversity and inclusion.

*    *    *

Brenda's concluding remarks echo that of Pat Milligan's in our Chapter 10 profile: If you want to advocate for gender equity in the workplace, you need to be smart in how you go about it.

Francis Ford Coppola said, "The way to come to power is not always to merely challenge the Establishment, but first make a place in it and then challenge and double-cross the Establishment."

While I'm not sure your motives need to be that nefarious, the point stands: To really effect change, first gather your power base. Even to begin collecting the data Brenda talks about here might be difficult. At the same time, you can equip yourself now to take advantage as soon as you see an opportunity to volunteer for a project, an initiative, or a program that advances gender equity.

Brenda's story about the well-meaning man who gave a low performance rating to the new mother highlights a great point that I hope you pick up again and again throughout this book: The vast majority of the bias against women is not intentional. Ladies, "The Man" isn't out to get us. Men are not the enemy. The enemy is the status quo, inertia, a lack of knowledge, a lack of urgency, a lack of understanding, and a lack of incentive.

# define your own success

*"I wish I'd had the courage to live a life true to myself,
not the life others expected of me."*

—Bronnie Ware, *Regrets of the Dying*

Don't say you want to empower women.

When you "empower" someone, it means you cede or grant them power—as if you owned it, as if it's yours to give or take away. Congress can empower the EPA to set environmental standards. A teacher can empower students to choose their own projects. A parent can empower a child to dress themselves. In those cases, a group or person has legitimate authority over another, whereby personal power is a privilege, not a right.

Don't say you want to empower me. You don't own my power. I don't need your permission to do what I want with it. You cannot grant what is already mine. I'm already empowered.

I can say that; my grandmother couldn't.

## A Narrow Escape from Genocide and the Fight for Our Power

My mother always told me that my great-grandfather died from a snakebite. It wasn't until a few years ago I found out the awful truth: He was corralled with other Armenian scholars at the university where he worked and murdered by Turkish military forces . . . just for being Armenian.

Why? The Ottoman Empire who governed Turkey at the time wasn't going to repeat the mistakes of the Hamidian massacres in the late 1800s, when the "bloody Sultan" Abdul Hamid II gave instructions to a paramilitary group to "deal with the Armenians as they wished." The ensuing massacres across Constantinople and the provinces left 100,000 to 300,000 Armenians dead. The killings ended partly because academics inside the country reached out to Western journalists and leaders to share news of the horrors, and many governments and organizations pressured Turkey to halt the slaughter.

Years later, when the government decided to pick up where it left off, it started with the intellectuals. On April 24, 1915, they arrested around 250 academics or other outspoken leaders, most of whom were later killed.

While fighting with the Central Powers against the Allies in World War I, the Turks began the Armenian Genocide in earnest.[1] They first killed the able-bodied men and then forced the elderly, women, and children on death marches into the desert. Scholars estimate that 1.5 million Armenians died during the genocide.

My great-grandfather wasn't among the first 250 academics killed; his death came during the later waves. They simply came to Euphrates College, pulled him and his fellow teachers outside, and shot them. One man escaped, ran back to the village where my great-grandmother lived to warn everyone and then disappeared into the mountains.

She knew the situation was hopeless. She sent her two oldest daughters (ages 13 and 14) to hide in the church with the rest of the villagers but hid her 9-year-old daughter under the floorboards and her infant daughter—my grandmother—in a bureau drawer. When the soldiers came, she met them at the door and somehow kept them from searching the house. They slaughtered her in the street.

When the soldiers came to the church, they threatened to burn it down as they had so many others. As the parishioners came out, they were either shot or imprisoned. My great-aunts, though, were offered a choice: Convert to Islam and become the wives of two older Turkish officers, or die. They chose to marry and became yet another of those officers' many wives. However, because of their choice, they saved their two younger sisters. The infant came to live with them, but the 9-year-old was forced to march into the desert, eventually making her way to a Syrian refugee camp.

My great-aunts were raped, brutalized, and abused. They soon gave birth to their own children, who were treated as half-breeds by the rest of the family. Despite this horrific life, they protected and provided for their youngest sister (my grandmother) and secretly brought her up in their own faith. They prayed to Allah in public and Christ in private.

Eventually, when my grandmother was about 5 years old, she and her second-oldest sister escaped with help from Turkish family friends. Their eldest sister stayed behind to raise her and her sister's children. The two joined their other sister in the Syrian refugee camp and all three eventually made their way to Massachusetts over the next decade and a half. As her family could not afford to take care of her when she arrived in the U.S. at the age of 19, my grandmother was put into an arranged marriage with my grandfather, who was in his early 30s at the time.

My grandfather was an angry man who physically and mentally abused my grandmother. In fact, one of my earliest memories is of him shoving my grandmother to the floor. By the time she was 40, my dear grandmother had had a psychotic break, perhaps catalyzed by the death of one sister as well as from years of trauma and abuse. She felt alone, afraid, and hopeless. My mother and her siblings were in grade school while their mother spent a year in a psych ward.

My mother missed an entire week of school because my grandfather said, "You've got to stay home and cook and take care of the house while your mother's away." My mother's brother went to school uninterrupted.

Years later, my mother married her childhood sweetheart. While my father was a typical military man in many ways, he loved my mother and us children. My mother put herself through a business certificate program and became a bookkeeper. She was a "working mother" before they even had a term for it.

An aunt once told me that my mother worked because she had to. I knew that wasn't true. She worked because it gave her freedom and independence. She wasn't going to live her life by the decisions of someone else.

My great-grandmother, the one who gave her life to save her children from the Turkish soldiers, named my grandmother Arshalous, Armenian for "dawn." In the midst of the Armenian Genocide, she believed her daughter would escape the darkness and find hope in the light of a new day.

I come from a long line of women whose lives and destinies were dictated by others. With each successive generation, though, they've struggled to gain some measure of control and had hope that the next generation would have it even better.

My mother instilled in me the ideals of independence, self-reliance, and self-determination. My father taught me about responsibility, sacrifice, and honor. Without realizing it—and despite my father's horror at the word—my parents raised a feminist.

I come from a family of women who sacrificed their very lives for their daughters, sisters, and nieces. Finally, Arshalous' granddaughter lives in a place and time where women can make their own choices and live their own lives.

I don't need your "empowerment." I've got my own.

## Find What Success Looks Like for You

It breaks my heart to know that few women have embraced the freedom they could have. They still let someone or something else control their fate and direction.

I'm talking about women who fulfill a so-called traditional role as well as the "emancipated women" who bought into the lie of being able to have it all. That is, the ones who want a high-flying career with a perfect marriage, perfect children, a perfect house, and the perfect body clad in perfect clothes and driving a perfect car. I feel sorry for any women forced into an expected role. There's no power in living someone else's version of your life.

Please stop to deeply consider this question: What do *you* want?

### From News Anchor to Spiritual Anchor

May I publicly declare how much I admire Liz Walker?

Originally from Little Rock, Arkansas, Liz worked her way up through TV newscasts from Denver to San Francisco before finally becoming the first black news anchor in Boston in 1981, a position she held for more than two decades. During that time she earned roughly half a million dollars a year and drew both criticism (for having a son out of wedlock, despite being an independent, self-made woman) as well as praise (for her investigative reporting of human trafficking in Sudan). Regardless of the circumstances, she has always carried herself with grace and humility.

She founded the nonprofit organization My Sister's Keeper, aimed at educating girls in war-torn countries. She helped found another Massachusetts-based anti-violence nonprofit. She's earned two Emmys for her work in journalism. She serves on the boards of a number of worthwhile causes.

Then, in the middle of her life, at the peak of her career, she just walked away. She earned a master of divinity degree from Harvard and then stepped down from journalism to step into the pastorate of Roxbury Presbyterian Church, located in one of Boston's most violent low-income neighborhoods.

The daughter of a minister herself, she said it was like "coming back." She was one of the leading voices calling for healing in the aftermath of the Boston Marathon bombing. She spearheads a trauma recovery project for the surrounding community and advocates for greater access to mental health-care services.

She left a prominent position and a powerful platform to go into a vocation she believes is her calling. She's changing the status quo and going against all expectations for someone of her public stature.

This isn't a retirement job. This is inner-city, mission-type, on-the-front-lines and in-the-trenches work with the most vulnerable, at-risk populations in Boston.

What a disrupter. What a woman.

Not every woman wants to be in the C-suite of a multinational. Not every woman wants to become a CEO. Not every woman wants to sit on the board of a publicly traded company.

Not every woman wants to be a wife. Not every wife wants to be a mother. Not every mother wants to be a wife. Not every woman even wants to be a woman.

I have worked in big tech for a long time. I also consult for large organizations to help them with gender-equity programs and with women who are leading large-scale change in environments that perpetuate bias, unconscious and otherwise, against women leaders.

I also coach women poised to become chief executives or board members. I'm an investor in women-led enterprises. More important, I'm a wife of 20-plus years and the mother of two wonderful daughters.

I'm a wife because I love a man named Chris. I'm a mother because I wanted to share this journey called life with my own children. I'm a leader because I can effect change. I'm an adviser because I want to help other leaders address serious inequities. I'm an investor because I want to do well while doing right. I am these things not because I'm expected to, but because they're what I've chosen to do.

I don't want you to be like me; I want you to be you.

Take one of my friends, Heather Boggini. She has the best of all worlds. No, she doesn't sit on the board of directors of a publicly traded company, she's not the CEO of her own startup, and she didn't spend years investing in her career or honing a skill or building a brand.

In fact, she doesn't even have a "real job"—not by the standards of the corporate world, anyway. She's devoted most of the past 20 years to raising her children and managing her household while her husband ran his commercial real estate development firm. These are skills I do not possess and have always admired. If Grand Central station ever needed a COO, Heather would be the ideal candidate.

But Heather also has an MBA from Northeastern University and co-founded a successful consultancy with me after deciding she wanted to end her long hiatus from the working world. She has taught herself most of what it takes to run our organization's daily operations.

What's most important is that Heather loves her life. She loves to work behind the scenes. She loves to make inappropriately funny remarks at inappropriate times. She has a thriving business and family. She has time for herself and time to do what she loves on her terms.

She didn't accept the traditional path the way it's "supposed to be done." That is, landing a job, working hard, and then moving up the ranks into management. Nor did she go the Silicon Valley route: Create a tech startup, get VC funding, grow the company, and then sell out. She didn't even take the route of creating a full-time business that she could grow and eventually retire from.

Heather didn't take a cue from anyone's playbook. She decided what she wanted, and then she created a life around that vision. She embodies one of the most fundamental principles of the women of *Disrupters*. When we talked about this book, she told me, "When it was time for me to return to work full time, I modeled women who were doing it successfully by integrating their work with their house and family responsibilities. I pulled from those examples what I thought would work for me. Was it easy? Heck no—but worth it."

In essence, she said, "Screw the way it's supposed to be done. I'm doing it my way." Heather owns her empowerment. Always has. Always will.

> "The world inside myself is vaster and richer than this paltry plane, peopled with mere galaxies and gods."
>
> —Rachel Hartman

## Make the Means Justify the End

This book isn't about how to climb the corporate ladder.

*Disrupters* is about the "how," not the "what." Yes, we'll talk a lot about women who've succeeded in business, evidenced by the lofty peaks they've conquered. There are comparatively fewer obstacles in your path if you want to homeschool your children or be a full-time volunteer. Those choices aren't any less valid or any less heroic than mine or Heather's or Oprah's.

*Disrupters* isn't about the destination. It's about how to get where you want to go. Everyone has a different finish line. Your challenge is to define yours.

> "You can waste your life drawing lines. Or you can live your life crossing them."
>
> —Shonda Rhimes

Or, if that's too vague, let me put it this way: You have options. You're not trapped. At least, not in the long term. I want to show you women who, when faced with an either/or choice, went a third way. They did the unexpected. They opted out of the machine.

They switched careers, they jumped companies, they went part time, they started their own companies or VC funds, they took the off-ramp for a couple of years and then got back their chosen track. They didn't find *the* way, but *their* way. And they were open to changing the path to their destinations when it no longer worked.

My friend Lisa Reeves cut her teeth in the enterprise technology market before moving over to venture capital. Both industries are notoriously male-dominated and overtly sexist. As a pragmatist with an insatiable hunger to build and disrupt, she became a General Partner at a venture firm focused on tech. After that, she became a vice president and general manager at Citrix's SaaS division. Lisa then cofounded the software company GridCraft, acquired in 2015 in a successful exit to Workday[2]. She is now Senior Vice President of Products at HR technology company Zenefits. She finds time to run marathons and truly enjoy her life. She created her own path on her own terms.

> **"Sometimes you find out what you are supposed to be doing by doing the things you are not supposed to do."**
>
> —Oprah Winfrey

One of my dissertation interviewees had a sister who graduated as an elementary school teacher. After a year, she realized that wasn't her life's calling. She quit to go work for a small company selling educational material.

After traversing the country for 19 years, she told her sister, "I've seen the inside of every hotel in America."

It hit her that she'd built up the lion's share of the customers and sales in the company. She approached the CEO and said she wanted equity in the company. He told her no.

She quit, found some financial backers, and launched her own educational publishing company. Twelve years later, she sold it in a multimillion-dollar deal.

The lesson here isn't that when you're told no to turn to entrepreneurship. That's simply one option among many. The takeaway is that these women didn't accept the way things were. Faced with a roadblock, they rerouted themselves.

There's more than one path to take during the race, but only one real way to win: Own your power. Define success for yourself and don't take no for an answer.

## Don't Play the Game Like a Man

In 1968, Professor Philip Goldberg tried an experiment about how gender and writing assessment intersect.[3] He handed out batches of essays to groups of his students, asking them to evaluate the work. The essays in each batch were identical; the one variable was the name at the top of the paper. Some had traditionally male names, while others had traditionally female ones. Across the board, the ones attributed to female authors scored lower than the identical ones attributed to males: the very definition of a double standard.

My doctoral research shows that although successful women recognize that this systemic bias exists, they also realize they can't control or seriously change it. Instead of ranting and railing about it, they focus on what they can do.

This often flies in the face of what we're told. Most diversity initiatives, mentoring programs, leadership advice, negotiating books, and the like tell women, in so many words, to look and act masculine.

The power-pump handshake, shoulder pads, those god-awful ties from years ago, wearing muted colors, being more aggressive in meetings, pushing harder—we're supposed to be less like women and more like men.

We're even expected to have the same sexual appetites.

In my first "real" career job (the previous ones had been planned stepping stones), the way people—and by that, I mean men—bonded was by saddling up to the bar or hanging at strip clubs. They would go drinking and then go to the clubs until three or four in the morning, go back to their hotel rooms, sleep for a few hours, and then go see the client.

I'd drink, but I didn't go with them to the XXX venues. While I didn't hold it against them and although they behaved as G-rated as you could at those spots, I could never stop thinking that the person up there on the pole was someone's sister or daughter. I'd always find some excuse: I needed to do some homework, I was working on another project, I didn't feel well, etc. While none of the guys ever said anything to my face, I would overhear remarks about those "other people" who never came out with them. I had to forgo camaraderie and some of my colleagues' goodwill because I felt their idea of a good time demeaned women. I was too junior and unsure of myself to voice my opinions to my much more experienced and successful colleagues. I was intimidated.

I don't believe that women (or men) should have to change who and what they are. While some flexibility is necessary—I haven't been married for more than 20 years by always getting my way—fundamentally changing our identity is not only unhealthy, it's wrong.

And useless.

A 2016 McKinsey study on women in the workplace found that even when women sought promotions as frequently as their male co-workers, they were statistically less likely to land the promotion (39 percent vs. 36 percent). [4] In fact, the study found that women who negotiate like a man are punished for their efforts. Women, despite being counseled to be more assertive like their male counterparts, are 30 percent more likely to receive feedback that they're intimidating, aggressive, or—my all-time favorite—"bossy."

While studying women seeking venture capital, the Diana Project found in 2014 that even when women pitch investors for capital like men, they still don't receive nearly as much funding. [5]

(This lack of funding isn't due to a lack of success. First Round Capital, which funded such startups as Uber, Mint, Square, and Blue Apron, found in their 2015 First Round 10 Year Project that out of 300 startups, female-founded companies outperformed all-male founding teams by 63 percent.[6])

Even when we act like men, we still don't experience the same kind of success. It's like the old saying: We have to work twice as hard to get half as much.

I just can't live my life trying to win a rigged game. I have too much I want to do to fight a losing battle (or, at best, a virtual stalemate). More important, I don't want my daughters to grow up in a world where all I've done for their generation is nudge the needle.

I don't want to fight—I want to *win*.

## Can't Win the Race? Change the Rules

So many women are running around, jumping from project to project or job to job, trying to get ahead. It's the Red Queen's race from Lewis Carroll's *Through the Looking-Glass*:

> "Well, in *our* country," said Alice, still panting a little, "you'd generally get to somewhere else—if you ran very fast for a long time, as we've been doing."
>
> "A slow sort of country!" said the Queen. "Now, *here*, you see, it takes all the running *you* can do, to keep in the same place. If you want to get somewhere else, you must run at least twice as fast as that!"

So many women I meet or mentor feel like Alice: It seems they've been running harder and longer than any of their male peers, but it doesn't look like they're really going anywhere.

At some point, we have to ask ourselves: Are we running a race worth winning? If we give it our all and make it to the finish line, will we be where we truly wanted to end up? Are we working toward what we really want? Or are we doing what we're "supposed to do," trying to prove that we can succeed in a man's world?

Just as important: Are we living a life worth living along the way? Are we pursuing a path that holds meaning for us individually? Do our lives—personally and professionally—align with the values we hold dear?

> **"They who dance are thought mad by those who hear not the music."**

—Unknown

Because you and I come from different backgrounds, have different genetics, and have lived different lives, our values necessarily don't look alike. Heather Boggini loves the life she's created. It aligns with her values. My life looks vastly different from hers, but I love it; it works for me and my loved ones.

Pat Milligan, who heads Mercer's When Women Thrive research project, told women at the 2017 Mobile World Congress in Barcelona that we have the power to open our own doors. She suggested that when going for an interview or negotiating for a new role or promotion, you should ask a couple of key questions:

- How will the company ensure that you make the same amount as your male colleagues?
- How will the direct line supervisor, supported by HR efforts, ensure that you can obtain career success?

When Milligan asked the audience if anyone had had that conversation at work, only one hand in the large, standing-room-only auditorium was raised. She had one more important piece of advice: "Trust me: the corporations need your talent way more than you need them. If you don't get specific details on how you will be paid equally to men, on how your career will be supported with access to opportunities and people in power, move on to a company who will provide it."

You could go find a company where other women had blazed a trail ahead of you, where women and their perspectives are wanted and welcomed: Xerox, IBM, Pepsi, Deloitte, Kellogg, CGTN America (formerly CCTV-America), KPMG, Abbott, and Accenture, just to name a few of the giants. You could go find companies that support a flexible work schedule and embrace the challenges of employees who have lives outside of work. You could be like Lisa Reeves or that elementary school teacher-turned-saleswoman-turned-businesswoman and go start your own company or consulting firm.

At the very least, you should find a company that aligns with your values. I couldn't work for Halliburton or ExxonMobil, for example. Without even knowing the culture (though I'd guess it was heavily masculine), their industries don't align with what I want to devote my career to. I don't want to spend my life helping companies extract oil. There's nothing wrong with that profession. In fact, geoscience-related industries are deeply important in the world, and I applaud the people trying to responsibly utilize our natural resources. I get that and I do geek out everyone once in a while about some geo-scientific finding or another, but it's just not my passion.

Early in my career, I had a senior colleague who was a wonderful mentor. She taught me the ins and outs of intricate, years-long international business transactions. As much as I enjoyed learning from her and supporting her, I eventually left that position once I realized that my job was to make her look good. I wasn't in a position to do anything meaningful, nor was I being encouraged to do so. I had stayed there for far too long, partly because I did not want to appear ungrateful but also, truth be told, because I doubted my ability to succeed without her.

My catalyst came when I realized that I wasn't put on this earth to fulfill someone else's dream. I made the conscious choice to leave that trajectory so I could find my own path to happiness.

> **"***You have a calling that exists only for you and that only you can fulfill.***"**
>
> —Naomi Stephan

When you look at a position or company that doesn't align with why you work so hard, why should you stay there? When facing a decision, ask yourself: Will this move me toward my vision or away from it? Am I being driven by my true self? Or by some external factor, self-imposed belief, or someone else's standard?

This idea of alignment between passion and profession—a mix of personal and professional pursuits that seamlessly blend together—is deeply important. Unfortunately, women often leave their job or the work force altogether when they realize their goals are impractical or outright impossible. But they do so without a clear idea of where they're headed.

> **"**This was an adequate enough performance, as improvisations go. The only problem was that my entire education, everything I had ever been told or had told myself, insisted that the production was never meant to be improvised: I was supposed to have a script, and had mislaid it.**"**
>
> —Joan Didion

Ladies, we must "entrepreneur" our careers. An entrepreneur believes, often in blind faith and through sheer will, that they will persevere and get where they want to go. They have a dream no one else can see, but it's a dream that's vivid for them. It breaks my heart to speak to women who've run into the glass ceiling or found themselves outside the boys' club and decided to give up on their dreams. They settle for something less because they believe they have to.

I couldn't. Perhaps I am a narcissist. Maybe my ambition spills into the realm of greed. Certainly I'm stubborn. I could just be crazy. Whatever the motivation, I could never find contentment in simply being . . . well, content. I always need to do more, be more, accomplish more. I often filled gaps because I saw they needed to be filled and was awarded the title or position later. In fact, I've rarely taken an existing position; most were created or adapted for the path I was already forging.

On the other hand, I've never been motivated by someone's criticism of me. I've heard about people who achieved what they did because they had to "prove it to them" or "show them I could do it." I don't know about you, but my life's purpose isn't to prove other people wrong about me. My motivation comes from somewhere deep inside, not from other people's projected insecurities.

Please take my word for it, along with the examples of the women in this book: You can create your own path to true fulfillment. You don't have to win "like a woman" or "like a man." You don't have to follow a traditional career path. You don't have to live by the measure of success as it's defined by society, your family, your friends, your employer, your clients, your ethnic group, or even your own gender. You don't have to tread the trail carefully marked out for you. You don't have to live within the societal, cultural, or corporate confines in which you find yourself. You can entrepreneur your career so that it aligns with your goals, your priorities, and your calling.

Early feminism morphed into the message that women could "have it all." But it's not about having it all. It's about making choices about what we really want, and then realizing that we don't have to change who we are to get it. We don't have to be a man to succeed in a man's world.

Play by your own rules. Find your own finish line.

> **"Usted es el narrador de su propia vida, y usted puede o no crear su propia leyenda."**
> *("You are the storyteller of your own life, and you can create your own legend or not.")*
>
> —Isabel Allende

# pariah to pioneer

A.J. is a typical Silicon Valley life sciences venture capitalist. A.B, M.D., Ph.D., and MBA from Harvard (with stops at Georgetown and Cambridge along the way). Then straight into directing corporate pharmaceutical research and into investing. Today, A.J.'s responsible for multiple VC portfolios worth hundreds of millions of dollars. This sounds like the resume of virtually every VC investor: white guys with lots of initials behind their names.

A.J., however, is from Sri Lanka.

And A.J. is a "she."

When Anula Jayasuriya graduated from Harvard's joint M.D./ Ph.D. program, she didn't go into academic medicine like she was supposed to. She opted for an MBA instead. Some of her contemporaries looked at that a little sideways, but it wasn't until she graduated that the depth of her betrayal became clear: she didn't go on to practice medicine.

Horror of horrors: she took a corporate job.

### *Not many medical doctors made that kind of leap at that time, right?*

I was literally seen as a traitor to medicine. Keep in mind, I was doing this in the '80s. HMOs were just on the rise and I realized that the medical profession was changing dramatically. I saw a great opportunity at the intersection of business and medicine, so I pursued it. But most everyone else saw me as somebody who took up a slot in medical training—a precious resource that I was throwing away—by going first into pharma and then into investing.

I lost contact with most of my colleagues in the medical and academic communities with whom I had worked for a very long time. They saw my decision as betraying my (and their) profession.

At the time, there was a chasm between medicine and business. From the business side, they saw the value of my medical background, but the medical community didn't see the value in collaborating with business. In those days, they were quite hostile to the idea. Over time, views softened and there was more receptivity to collaboration between medicine and industry. Today, it's the norm. Now even Harvard has a joint M.D./MBA program! I'm fortunate in my own personal history to have been vindicated that I made the right decision. My friends today joke that I went from being a pariah to a pioneer. For a long time, though, it was a lonely, difficult journey.

The important thing to me is that I did what I felt was right. I believed that collaboration between those two communities would help society. I'm so happy to see that it has taken place.

### *Why is VC funding for female entrepreneurs important?*

There is a social justice angle, but more powerful than that is the fact that our society, composed of 51 percent female, is being systematically deprived of the insights, observations, and management styles of women. We have all these studies that show the power of diversity. Of course, women's and men's management styles fall along a spectrum. It is not black and white. But if you look at the mean distribution, you see very different management styles and approaches to leadership between genders.

By the majority of funding going to men, we're missing out on the different ways a woman might innovate than a man, or the different products and services women would create that many men simply wouldn't see.

None of that comes to the fore if women aren't given the first step of funding and contributing their different viewpoints, be it on the product itself or in the leadership of the company.

The real question is: By not funding these women, what are we missing out on?

***Why doesn't the empirical data demonstrating the financial returns of women-led or women-founded startups and businesses seem to compel the investment community to add more of those companies to their portfolios?***

I think it comes down to several things, one of which is that the venture community isn't quite . . . driven by facts, shall we say?

In the grand scheme of things, it's actually quite small, like a cottage industry. The amount of money is significant, but in terms of the number of people making decisions, it's quite a small, elite club.

People have their own individual styles of investing: what they want to invest in, what they don't, who they trust, etc. Everyone has their own internal algorithm, but it really comes down to human nature.

Venture investing isn't like public equity investing. With a publicly traded company, you have metrics and performance data to assess. Venture capital is about assessing ideas and, more importantly, the people behind the idea.

A venture investment decision involves spending a lot of time with entrepreneurs. You need to understand them, to relate to them, and to really get inside their head. You want to be able to trust the person to whom you're entrusting limited partners' capital [the institutions that typically invest in venture funds]. You have a fiduciary responsibility to your LPs. You want to have faith in these people that they know what they're doing and that they're going to do the right thing. It's much easier to do that if they're like you.

It shouldn't surprise us that if nine out of every ten venture capitalists are male, the majority of venture capital would go to the people who look, act, and think like them. That's biology: We're wired to connect with and trust the people for whom we have an affinity, and we have an affinity for those most like us.

Another factor is that we invest in places where we've had or seen success before. If most of your successes come from your male-led teams, then you're probably going to gravitate to similar teams.

### What about your own funding algorithm?

When it comes to backing entrepreneurs, I have two passions.

One is in seeing an increase in the number of successful women entrepreneurs. Ultimately, it's not just about the funding. That's just an intermediate goal. The real goal I have in mind is getting them to succeed: to have them influence society with their products as well as their leadership.

My other passion is women's health. In that sphere, the innovators are overwhelmingly women. There are some men serving the health needs, but again, women are uniquely suited to address the gap in the market for these products and services.

As a woman myself, I have a different perspective than my male counterparts about whether an entrepreneur has identified a potential market that addresses women, whether that entrepreneur's team can deliver, and whether the product meets that need. I can more ably assess the opportunity than someone unfamiliar with the market.

Fifty-one percent of the population is female, yet women's health has been chronically underserved for decades. Women can more easily relate to these unmet needs and gaps in the market. Silicon Valley likes to call this space "femtech," though I must admit I'm not sure I love the term. It's clearly more attractive than "women's health," which is quite a clunky term, though more factual and much broader. Femtech, in its current use, centers around reproductive health—fertility and infertility—and doesn't include the other major areas of women's health. Having said that, I welcome any kind of progress, whether by women entrepreneurs or by innovations brought to the market that serve women's health and wellness.

Lastly, I'm also a Ph.D. scientist, so I can evaluate the data behind the products. I do most of my own due diligence: I know whom to contact for a certain area of women's health to talk about the medical science of a product or market.

### *What should female entrepreneurs know about getting VC funding?*

Have you seen that article in the *Harvard Business Review* about the Swedish VCs talking differently about male and female entrepreneurs? When assessing a man, the investors would say they were "young and promising," whereas they would describe a woman as "young and inexperienced." Despite similarities between the male-led and female-led ventures, the VCs systematically saw the men as a better opportunity.

I'm sure some of this is from how we're wired, as I said previously, but I also think that male VCs have to recalibrate themselves when listening to a woman pitch.

The male entrepreneur paradigm is to come into a VC presentation with the line "This is going to be a billion-dollar company! We're going to do X, Y, and Z! We're going to disrupt the whole industry!" and all these other fabulous things that will happen. Exaggeration is expected. It's called "thinking big!"

If everyone you hear is saying they're going to change the world and then this woman comes along and circumspectly says, "We can reasonably expect this kind of growth, we project these kinds of returns, and we're going to help a lot of people in the process" . . . well, an investor who's been listening to people pitching moon shots doesn't know how to place this realistic presentation. They're not calibrated for this different style of leadership, communication, and management.

So there are two options for women to succeed in an industry that's calibrated more for males. One is to adopt the male style of pitching VCs. If someone's comfortable doing that, then that's fine, but if not, I don't advocate this approach. I think you need to be comfortable and you need to have integrity. Otherwise, you're not being true to yourself and you're compromising your integrity.

The best solution is for the investors to recalibrate how they view and evaluate women entrepreneurs. One way to achieve that is to have women in the decision-making process to help align the investors and the female presenters.

The other option is for women to compensate for this misalignment with exceptional preparation. (By the way, I give this same advice to men as well.) Do their homework on the investors they're approaching. Try to discover what companies are in their portfolio. Look at the firm overall: What kind of ventures do they usually back? What areas of the entrepreneur overlay with any areas they've shown interest in before? How does their product or service fit into the firm's history of investments?

Take a look at the founders and teams who've successfully pitched to them in the past. How did they approach the investor? What's their style? Take a look at the makeup of those teams: Were there any women? Are there any signals that this investor is more calibrated to women than other VCs?

That way, when pitching them, you can make those connections for them: "You're already familiar with this field because of your involvement with X company." "This is similar to a company already in your portfolio, which does Y."

The VC industry is in the dark ages and in urgent need of radical change. I believe that until the number of women investors and women investees equal men, the playing field will remain skewed to the detriment of the economy and society. That is why organizations like Astia—on whose board I served for a decade and whose mission is to enable high-growth women entrepreneurs to access the networks and expertise needed for their success—are essential to turbocharging this change.

*It's inspiring to hear how you've pursued this vision of helping women, despite being a "pariah" to your profession. I think a lot of women can relate: being a traitor to their own professions, to their culture, to their religions, to their families, or whatever it is that they break from to pursue what they believe is right for them.*

I don't want to pretend that I had a clear compass and knew what was happening. It wasn't like I was Joan of Arc fighting through adversity. I made several missteps and stubbed my toe on many dead ends. Personally, I feel fortunate that it mostly worked out. Above all, I'm glad that there is widespread understanding that basic science, clinical medicine, and the pharmaceutical industry must collaborate.

But I do want to emphasize that it's not about me feeling vindicated. I could have been vindicated about a path I took that turned out to be bad for society. I'm vindicated because this has been about what's best for patients, for women, and for the world.

↗  ↗  ↗

Let me point out the ways in which Anula typifies a disrupter.

First and foremost, she bucks the status quo. Despite being shunned by her friends and colleagues in medical circles, she pursued what she believed was the future.

You've heard Wayne Gretzky's quote about the secret to his success, right? "I skate to where the puck is going to be, not to where it has been." Anula embodies that idea. She saw the opportunity for collaboration between business and medical science and put herself squarely in that intersection ahead of the curve.

You can see that she has a deep sense of purpose. She makes million-dollar decisions that, in addition to being prudent investments, also advance her mission of making the world a better place through women's health.

She gets that investing in women isn't just a social justice issue but an economic issue as well. Companies do better, economies perform better, and overall socioeconomic opportunities are better when women compete on the same level as men. To put a fine point on it: promoting women isn't just good for women—it's good for society.

Lastly, I love her humility. While she says it feels nice to see that she made the right choices, despite everyone in her professional network warning her against that path, her gratification doesn't come from being able to prove them wrong. Her fulfillment comes from feeling that she set out to do the right thing for the world and seeing that come to pass.

THREE

# choose career
# *and* family

*"Feminism wasn't supposed to make us miserable. It was supposed to make us free . . . The challenge lies in recognizing that having choices carries the responsibility to make them wisely, striving not for perfection or the ephemeral all, but for lives and loves that matter."*

—Debora Spar

"I find no data to support any other conclusion than women leave because they want to raise their family. That's what the data shows."

I heard these words from the mouth of a male software engineer, an embodiment of the "it's not me, it's you" mentality. Many men believe fewer of us reach the top because we leave before we get there. We want to be wives and mothers. The gender gap is our fault.

There is a sliver of truth to that sentiment. A 2015 McKinsey & Co. study[1] found that just 60 percent of senior female managers aspire to chief executive vs. 72 percent of men at the same level. Fewer women than men want to be CEO.

But it isn't because they want to go have a family instead.

When the study asked both sexes why they didn't want the top spot, almost the same percentage of men as women cited a desire to balance work and family (65 percent vs. 62 percent, respectively).

> **"*Feminism isn't about making women stronger. Women are already strong. It's about changing the way the world perceives that strength.*"**
>
> —G.D. Anderson

If it isn't because they want to go home and raise their family, what is it? Maybe it's because women don't have the same motivation as men—we're underrepresented at the top because we have less ambition to get there. That must be the difference, right?

If that were true—if ambition were the key—then the S&P 500 would be led by a small army of black women. A 2015 report by the Center for Talent Innovation titled "Black Women: Ready to Lead,"[2] found that 22 percent of black professional women want a powerful position with a prestigious title vs. just 8 percent of their white counterparts.

Going strictly by those numbers, black women should outnumber white women in the upper echelons of business by almost three to one. They don't, of course. In fact, of the 26 women who are currently CEOs of the S&P, none is black. (There was one—Ursula Burns at Xerox—but she stepped down in 2016.)

As I mentioned earlier, mothers are *more* likely to aspire to be chief executive than their childless colleagues (38 percent vs. 24 percent). Obviously, a lack of ambition isn't what's keeping women back.

So what is it?

# Read Only If You're a Man with a Daughter

A male acquaintance of mine told me when he finally got it:

*I was walking my newborn daughter back and forth across the room, singing her a lullaby. After she fell asleep in my arms, I gazed for a long time at her face, wondering what the future held for my little princess. Would she grow up to become an artist? A ballet dancer? An entrepreneur? A take-charge CEO?*

*As my imagination wandered around, I thought about the challenges of her working in a corporate environment, as I once did. I thought about how my old boss treated women. I thought about my little girl being denied a promotion by someone like him because she wasn't one of his usual hires.*

*The more I thought about it, the madder I got. I became incensed. I muttered to myself—not loud enough to wake her—that I'd be damned if a little arrogant punk tried to keep my daughter down. I'd be damned if he tried to put her "in her place"! I'd be damned if my perfect daughter was denied her dreams just because of what was or wasn't between her legs!*

*And in that moment . . . I got it. I finally understood feminism.*

The men I've met who get it—who see the disconnection and believe it must change—all have this one thing in common: they have a daughter or a granddaughter.

It's a different story when something happens to someone we love. Racism is an abstract concept . . . until someone you care about is called a racial slur. Crime statistics are just numbers . . . until your spouse is robbed at gunpoint. Health-care reform is just a political issue . . . until your sibling with cancer loses his job.

And when the woman or girl in your life gets the door slammed in her face before she can even open it, or when she hits the glass ceiling or sees a man pass her on the glass escalator, suddenly equity and access aren't just abstract concepts to be lightly dismissed. But this is the daily reality for women everywhere. That's why we're working toward a new world where all talent can thrive equally.

## We Know We're a Lot of Trouble #sorrynotsorry

The same German manager who "saw no data" had a color-coded list of all his direct reports. When he was considering tasking someone with spearheading a new project or initiative, he'd refer to the list—and then skip all the names highlighted in pink, mine included.

I once asked him, "What does the pink represent?"

Nonchalantly, he said, "Oh, those are all you women in your childbearing years. I don't want to give you a yearlong project and then have you drop out nine months into it because you're having a baby."

Oh. My. God. Blatant, casual sexism—literally in pink!

Then, of course, you have former Harvard University president Lawrence Summers publicly stating in 2005 that, faced with the choice of family or doing the work it takes to get to the top in science and engineering, women choose to not sacrifice family time. This was the same man who said that boys outperform girls in math and science because of biological differences.

(Unsurprisingly, during his presidency, the number of tenure offers to female professors fell by two-thirds . . . but that can be explained by genetics, right?) What a difference a change in leadership makes; at a press conference in 2007, regarding her appointment as

Harvard's first female president, Drew Faust said, "I'm not the woman president of Harvard. I'm the president of Harvard." We don't have to qualify the position by gender. One of the ways I'll know that we've arrived at gender equity is when we stop saying "female high-growth entrepreneurs" and "women CEOs."

Of course there are biological differences between men and women. Besides the common-sense ones (obviously men don't have ovaries), we've already discussed some of the research showing the differences between the sexes, such as the different motivations each have.

But did Summers truly believe that high school boys outperform girls in math because they're inherently smarter? That's the same type of logic racists used in the 1900s to "prove" that black people were genetically inferior to whites. While speaking about African economic development in 2007, Nobel laureate scientist James Watson said: "All our social policies are based on the fact that their intelligence is the same as ours—whereas all the testing says not really." *In 2007.*

Do girls score lower because they just don't have what it takes? Or is it because they have teachers and parents who think like him? Authority figures who continually reinforce the idea that females are somehow "less"?

On the reason why women don't aspire to the top, though, Summers is right. The number-one reason they gave in the 2016 McKinsey report on women in the workplace: "I wouldn't be able to balance family and work commitments." Although I hate to burst his testosterone-filled bubble, that's also the number-one reason men gave in the same survey.

The real trouble with women is . . . we're too much trouble.

## The Leaky Pipe of Corporate Talent

Part of the reason women don't reach the top *is* because we're leaving before we ever get there. We're opting out of corporate and starting our own gigs. And a lot of it is because of family matters—but it's only because we're a square peg that can't fit into a round hole.

The brass usually identifies potential rising stars when those up-and-comers are in their 40s. By this point, they've had enough time to gain competency and demonstrate leadership ability. Unfortunately for women, our 40s are often just when our families need us most. Our children are often in their demanding teenage years, our parents' and loved ones' health issues begin to surface, and we're often undergoing the change of life. (I fall into this category myself.) In fact, sociologists often refer to people in their 40s and 50s (usually in Western countries) as the "sandwich generation." At least one in ten of Americans in this age bracket are simultaneously caring for a child and a parent, while similar situations have been observed in Australia and the U.K., according to the Pew Research Center's 2013 report "The Sandwich Generation."[3]

A 2004 study by R.F. Roffer found[4] that women left senior leadership positions—that is, the point when people are traditionally poised to rise into the C-suite—because of obstacles in their career path or outright gender bias. McKinsey's 2017 "Women in the Workplace"[5] found that the same number of women and men plan to quit their jobs in the next two years: 27 percent vs. 26 percent, respectively. More importantly, virtually the same number are leaving for identical reasons: leaving to go work for someone else (72 percent vs. 73 percent) or leaving the work force altogether to focus on family (2 percent vs. 1 percent). In short, many women are abandoning their positions at a traditionally critical point but not because we want to go home and take bubble baths every day.

Partly it's because we're pulled in a million directions. We have to engage in child care and/or elder care as well as take care of the household. As such, we're far less likely to pursue positions that would take us away from those duties. The 2016 gender gap study by the World Economic Forum[6] found that, globally, women work an average of 39 more days a year than men. We work almost an extra six weeks. The vast majority of that is unpaid, either from being the primary caretakers of family or—for those of us with formal employment—from the infamous second shift we all work after getting home . . . from work.

Want us to participate in the economy like men? Come back to us in our 50s. We're ready to go. We're awesome then. We have our ducks in a row. But if you haven't been marked and mentored by 50, the conventional wisdom is that you've already missed out. It's like the old days when you weren't married by 20: everyone knew you were going to be an old maid destined to die alone.

**"*You don't have to be anti-man to be pro-woman.*"**

—Jane Galvin-Lewis

McKinsey's 2012 "Women Matter" survey[7] took a look at the leaky pipeline problem. In analyzing those numbers, Harrier Human Capital found that men were three times as likely to be promoted to middle management than women, twice as likely to be promoted to senior management, and five times as likely to be promoted to CEO. Again, women are losing in the corporate world because we're playing a game with rules written for the guys. This is simply the reality. Women do have it harder.

But what are we to do? Eschew love, friends, and family so we can succeed in business? Take a humdrum job so we'll be there for our loved ones? Do we just accept the fact that we can have career or family but not both?

Sophie Vandebroek didn't.

## Refuse to Lose

As a 7-year-old girl in Belgium, she watched as humanity first walked on the moon. From then on, she dreamed of being an astronaut. The closest thing to an astronaut degree she could find was a double major in electrical and mechanical engineering. After that, she pursued a master's and then a Ph.D.

While she didn't become an astronaut, she did find professional fulfillment in her research, which eventually landed her a job at Xerox in 1991. Fast-forward five years: she had a loving husband (who she'd dated since she was 17), three wonderful children, and a fulfilling career. Her husband used to tell her that she had "the world by a string."

Then tragedy struck. While on a camping vacation, he suffered an asthma attack and died. In the space of 30 minutes, Sophie went from having it all to being a widow with three young children.

Life got tough, between juggling leadership and project responsibilities at a Fortune 500 company, raising three children who had lost their father, and taking care of herself.

Not only did she survive, she thrived. In 2006 (three years before Ursula Burns became CEO), Xerox offered her the prominent position of CTO. By that time, the company was no longer just manufacturing copy machines. About half of all revenue came from business services. Xerox had always been an innovative company (they actually invented key technologies of desktop computing, the mouse, and the graphic user interface that became the basis for Windows). After years of losing competitive ground, the corporation had begun to aggressively reassert itself in the early 2000s.

In short, being CTO of such a company was nothing short of an amazing opportunity. Moreover, a position like that would put Sophie in striking distance of becoming CEO one day.

The position, though, would necessarily require far more of her attention. Xerox was a global company with major operations centers all over the world, from its headquarters in Connecticut and main offices in Rochester, New York, to its research centers in France and India. Hiring babysitters and juggling kids' soccer practice around business meetings was one thing. Being a C-suite executive for a global company was a whole other ball game.

She was faced with the classic choice: career or family?

This is where many people point to the drop-off in female participation in the upper ranks. To run with the big boys, you have to forsake sitting down to play with your little boys.

Sophie made a career-killing move: She refused. Despite her lifelong ambitions; despite the opportunities such a position would afford; despite the win it would be for women in science, technology, engineering, and math roles; and despite the potentially world-changing technologies she would influence, she said no. That is . . . unless she didn't have to travel more than an hour's flight from her home in Boston.

Xerox agreed.

As a result, Sophie became responsible for hundreds of millions of dollars in assets and thousands of employees, and yet was always home for dinner. In fact, she did such a superb job that she later also became president of the company's prestigious five global research centers. Again, this move was in line with her family priorities: She has a son studying in Europe and a daughter in San Francisco, so when she travels for Xerox, she stays over extra days to spend time with them.

Sophie rewrote the rules of the game. Everybody won.

> **"I could not, at any age, be content to take my place by the fireside and simply look on. Life was meant to be lived. Curiosity must be kept alive. One must never, for whatever reason, turn his back on life."**
>
> —Eleanor Roosevelt

## The Myth of Work-Life Balance

Could you get away with that at your company? You may not be in a position to dictate terms. The takeaway, though, isn't that Sophie won a concession from Xerox. The lesson is that, faced with two options, she created a third. Instead of making the choice between family and work, she chose what I call whole life integration.

There's no such thing as work-life balance. I doubt there ever was. The women I've studied and worked with over the years don't approach their life in terms of balance. Balance is like a set of scales or a seesaw: When one side goes up, the other goes down. It's a one-for-one trade-off, an either-or proposition. When you think along those lines, you cut off your options. Your choices come down to black and white, A or B.

The women who break the rules don't think of it as choosing one or the other. Like Sophie, they find a way to have both. Grant me poetic license, but they weave their personal and professional lives into a harmonious whole. Why can't you work from home two or three days a week? Why can't you block out certain hours to take care of yourself? Why can't you move a standing meeting?

Sophie had an advantage: Xerox was already a woman-friendly company. From 2009 to 2016, Xerox's Ursula Burns was the S&P 500's only black female CEO, but Ursula's predecessor at Xerox was also a woman, Anne Mulcahy, appointed in 2000 to save the company from the brink of bankruptcy. In fact, the Mulcahy-Burns transition was the first woman-to-woman handoff in the history of America's global giants. At Xerox, women hold or have held the positions of CEO, CTO, CIO, CFO, and CMO. Additionally, women compose about 40 percent of the engineering division's new hires in the U.S.

Xerox doesn't have a leaky pipe problem.

Do you think it's because they naturally attract more women willing to forgo child-rearing to soldier on for the company? Or do you think it's because their culture is better suited to the way women play the game?

If you want to devote yourself exclusively to raising your children and serving your family, then by all means do so. If you want to create a wonderful medley of family, professional, and social activities like Heather Boggini, that's great, too. If you want to create change inside your company or launch your own startup, requiring long hours of focus and effort, go for it. But don't buy into the lie that you must choose between fulfillment on the job or at home.

Women get blamed because we're supposed to take care of the household, the kids, our husband, and the dog. If we do one thing, we're taking away from something else. That old-school mentality forces a dichotomy: you can either feel guilty about subverting your career and stalling your ambitions, or you can feel guilty about not spending time at home and putting your job ahead of your family.

Either way, we're supposed to feel guilty.

It's not easy, but you can find a way to have both. The women I've observed use a number of strategies, singly or together, to win at the whole work-life thing.

> **"When you know better, you do better."**
>
> —Maya Angelou

## Plan Smart Transitions

Our rule breakers don't buy into the either/or myth. They recognize that life is complex and ever changing. What works for them right now won't work in 15 years (or even 5).

Instead of choosing one route or the other, they weave and swerve between the traffic cones. They may need to ramp down while they care for their parents or attend to a personal matter, but at the right time, they ramp up and get back in the fast lane.

Men are doing this, too. Mike, a friend of mine, is a divorced father of two. When his mother developed terminal cancer, he took off work to care for her during the last two years of her life but later reentered the work force. He says it was the best decision he ever made. Sure, he "left" his day job, but he didn't opt out entirely; he just ramped down for a little while.

Women who've done this say they didn't shut the door entirely either. They still went to lunch with colleagues, attended the occasional conference, and kept up their certifications or added skill sets to their repertoire. Sometimes they took on consulting gigs or did some freelance work. They never closed the door to full-time employment. They always left it open a crack—at least enough to keep their foot in the door.

Ilyssa Frey, director of communications for the alumnae program at Wellesley College, took a break from her budding communications career in technology to raise her twins. She had every intention of returning to work once they were in school, so she kept up her connections through periodic email exchanges, lunches, and coffees.

As she navigated toward earning a paycheck again, she used these skills to land a key communications role in a new industry: academia.

Disrupters embrace the "and."

## Maintain Strict Boundaries

But some rule breakers are sticklers for self-imposed rules.

During my dissertation research, one of the venture capital world's most powerful women told me, "When people want me to mentor them, I make them walk with me. I don't do lunch meetings and I don't go other places; I make them come to my house. They walk up the hill with me as I exercise. So if you look at my calendar, I've got a walk scheduled almost every day with someone—usually a woman, but sometimes a man—from different companies and organizations."

This is a classic superwoman: a generous heart married to a focused vision. She freely gave advice and counseling to those in need, but on her terms and her turf. She was strict about prioritizing her health and well-being—she was religious about her daily walks up and down the hill—but as long as she could accomplish her goals, she was willing to help however she could.

A C-suite technology executive who sits on several public and private company boards told me she simply turned her email off and completely unplugged from work one day a week. By carving out that peaceful haven every week, she could focus on her other priorities: herself, her family and social life, and her personal pursuits. She realized that if she didn't create that space, no one else would do it for her.

She and others like her fight Parkinson's law: Work expands so as to fill the time available for its completion. But instead of allowing work to consume them, they place it inside a boundary and force it—whether it takes the form of paperwork, favors, responsibilities, projects, or anything else—to stay within those boundaries.

In fact, Clay Christensen, author of *The Innovator's Dilemma* and *How Will You Measure Your Life?*, said that these kind of boundaries are what separated him from the Enron and WorldCom guys, many of whom were his friends. He said that, truthfully, they weren't villains—they just lost sight of what was important and became consumed by greed. Clay, raised as a devout Mormon, never works on Sunday. Even in college as a basketball player, if the team had a game on Sunday, they'd have to play without him. He flat out refused.

## Embrace Flexibility

A pioneering disrupter I spoke with told me about how she had approached work-life integration years ago as the wife of a cardiac surgeon. She wanted to start her own business so he quit his job to be a stay-at-home dad while she pursued entrepreneurship.

In the 1970s.

She was adamant about them eating dinner together as a family, even though she routinely traveled or worked late into the evening. Her solution? Their nanny would care for the children during the day and put them to bed in the late afternoon. Then their dad would wake the kids up once their mom got home, and they'd all eat dinner at 9:30 every night.

We can't all have a nanny (I certainly don't), but you can find ways to achieve the outcome you want. It just may take you redefining the way you attain it. Instead of trying to conform to convention, this family turned tradition on its head. While plenty of people would call it crazy, it worked for them. She got to follow her dream of entrepreneurship and spend quality time with her husband and children every day. (Evening. Whatever.)

Flexibility is my strategy, too. Some days I have to do more professional activities than personal ones. Other days it's the opposite. I no longer say "working from home" because that treats the issue as a dichotomy: professional things can be done only at work, and personal things can be done only at home. Instead, I say "personal" or "professional," because my location doesn't matter. When I have to take care of a personal matter at the office, I haven't crossed some forbidden yet invisible boundary; I've just had to deal with something personal in a professional setting. I always have my laptop with me and routinely handle professional tasks while in a personal setting. I might work on a presentation in the doctor's waiting room while I take one of my daughters for a checkup.

An analysis of the 2005–2015 American Community Survey by the U.S. Census Bureau[8] found that half of the U.S. work force could work remotely and more than a fifth does it frequently. Furthermore, 80 to 90 percent of the respondents wish they could work remotely two to three days a week, focusing on "concentrative work" at home and then "collaborative work" at the office.

I don't seek "balance," whatever that is. I live my life, pursue my goals, and find a way to weave what I need and want to do around each other.

> **"I remember being in a group of old money trophy wives. They expressed sympathy that I 'had to have a job' and admonished me on how much I was missing. They told me how sorry for me they were. I didn't try to explain because they wouldn't get it: being a mom is just not enough for me. I love my work. When my family comes to my house and sees everything askew, they look at me sideways: I'm supposed to feel guilty about what they see as a pigsty. It seems no matter where I turn, I'm always supposed to feel embarrassed about who I am and the choices I've made."**
>
> —Anonymous

## Don't Hide Your Family

It makes me sick to recall, but I'm guilty of this.

When I was pregnant with one of my girls, my boss was rich, white, and older to the point that he truly couldn't understand why during maternity leave I constantly checked in and contributed to ongoing projects as much as I could. To add to the difficulty, he was German, a country where, at the time, men were traditional in their concept of female-male roles in the home. He also lacked empathy for what it was like to be an American worker in a global organization; when headcount cuts were made, they were done in the U.S., where at-will employment meant zero job security, regardless of performance. It was nearly impossible to relieve many of my European and Asian peers from their posts, due to local employment laws.

One time he said, "What's wrong with you? You're on leave. Why don't you just take care of your baby?"

I said, "I need to make sure my job's waiting for me when I get back. I'm the only breadwinner in my family. This isn't just my career—this is my family's means of living."

## The Rise of the Breadwinning Mother

According to the Pew Research Center's 2013 report "Breadwinner Moms,"[9] 40 percent of all U.S. households with children are led by mothers who are the sole or primary breadwinner in the family. Of those, about a third are married or in a long-term partnership, meaning that about two-thirds are single. But the difference between single mothers and married ones is stark: a median income of $23,000 vs. $80,000.

Meanwhile, across the pond, Europe isn't far behind. The Institute for Public Policy Research's "Who's Breadwinning in Europe?" (2015)[10] finds that in Britain, one in three of all households with children are headed by a woman who is the sole or primary breadwinner; in Germany, it's more than a quarter. Europe overall sits at about 31 percent. Unlike the U.S., the two types of breadwinning mothers in the U.K. and Germany are divided evenly: about half are single mothers and half are in a partnership.

Coming from his world of privilege and masculine tradition, he truly couldn't grasp my worry about what would happen if my job weren't waiting for me when I came off maternity leave. Due to these fears, I (shamefully) downplayed my family. I didn't want my superiors to get the impression that I might leave at any moment. I didn't want my name color-coded in pink on someone's roster of "women who might quit to go have a family."

This type of environment leads to a culture where women don't keep pictures of their kids on their desk. They don't want their boss or co-workers to worry about them choosing their family over their job. They almost feel compelled that their office communicates a message of "Don't worry about me dropping everything to go take care of a skinned knee, sir! I'm completely devoted to the job!"

If that's the culture you find yourself in, you should ask yourself some questions:

- Why do you feel compelled to hide or downplay a huge part of your life and identity?
- If you're in a culture that frowns on you having to attend to your personal commitments, is that really a company you want to work for?

These days, I've overcome my fears. I don't hesitate to share a cute story about my daughters or whip out a picture of my family. If I'm in a culture that discourages me from talking about this source of my joy, then I need to find a place that welcomes me as a whole human being.

## Have a Solid Foundation

Here's something nearly all my research participants had in common, and I've seen this in nearly all the disrupters I've admired since: They had a strong, solid, social foundation (i.e., a wonderful home life and/or community of personal and professional support). That usually meant a husband or partner with whom they had a wonderful relationship, a peaceful place to retreat from the world, and/or a close group of friends and family.

# Don't Ask, Don't Tell

There's a term for this kind of thing: *covering*. Covering happens when you minimize some part of yourself or your identity.

The classic example is FDR not allowing photographers to take pictures of him using leg braces or his wheelchair. While everyone knew that the president was unable to walk, he still wanted to downplay it as much as possible.

Today, covering is understood along four axes:

1. *Appearance*—such as someone from a lower socioeconomic background conspicuously displaying name-brand accessories or taking pains to avoid sunlight to keep their skin as light as possible

2. *Affiliation*—such as a mother not displaying pictures of her children at work or an Asian woman not relating a story about her recent car wreck

3. *Advocacy*—such as a Muslim not voicing her concerns about the travel ban or a person with a mentally disabled brother not challenging a joke about Forrest Gump

4. *Association*—such as an Indian ignoring overtures of friendship from Indian colleagues or a gay man consciously avoiding other gay men

The 2013 Deloitte study "Uncovering Talent: A New Model of Inclusion"[11] revealed that 61 percent of people cover on at least one axis of their life; two-thirds of all women do. Why? Because they feel that not covering—that is, more fully embracing that aspect of their identities—would put them at a disadvantage in their career.

Worse still, more than half the survey respondents say their leaders expect employees to cover (consciously or not), and nearly half said the organization overall had a culture that expected covering.

One executive, unmarried and without a partner, had a small farm outside Silicon Valley where she would retreat every weekend, from Friday until Sunday evening. That's where she would recharge—sometimes with her friends and family, sometimes on her own—and then wade back into the fray come Monday morning.

Justice Ruth Bader Ginsburg said of her lifelong husband, Martin, "I betray no secret in reporting that, without him, I would not have gained a seat on the Supreme Court." A lawyer himself, he moved from New York City to Washington, DC, for her career and sold off business interests that might have been deemed a conflict of interest. You could say he gave up his pursuits for his wife, but in a true partnership, I think it's more about support than sacrifice.

My own husband, Chris, has been a stay-at-home dad since our oldest child, Annabella, was born. We didn't plan it that way. Once we had Annabella, we reevaluated our lives and decided that was how we wanted to live. (He's been amazing, by the way.) He isn't particularly career-driven; I am. He wanted his job to be our family. This arrangement works for us. The point is that we had a choice. If he had wanted to remain in the work force, we would have made different choices, although I'm not sure I would have had the flexibility to do all the wonderful things I have been able to take part in. For us, it was an easy decision. For others, it is not. That's not fair.

That's not to say you need a partner to be successful. Sophie Vandebroek found success as a widower and single mother (though she's now happily married again). I'd never argue that you need a

# The Disruptettes

"If women want equal rights, they can open their own
damn doors!"

—Author's father, an unwitting feminist

My mother didn't know she was a feminist. My father didn't know he was one either. Neither of them knew that they raised me to be one. Truth be told, I didn't even know I was a feminist until I pursued my doctorate.

Being a feminist doesn't mean that I don't want my husband to open the occasional door for me (which he does). It means we acknowledge that women should have equal access, equal freedoms, and equal opportunities. I want to see the needle move in my lifetime, but you know who I hope benefits most?

Our daughters.

As I related previously, in my experience (and the research bears me out), male senior executives don't "get the whole women's thing" until they have a daughter or even a granddaughter. Not a wife, a mother, or a sister. Female offspring. It takes that relationship for the reality to sink in that their daughters won't have the same opportunities and access as their sons.

I especially don't understand women who've had a job, experienced the disparity in business culture firsthand, and still don't get it. A woman in my inner circle once told me me, "I don't really care about what you're doing. I'm done with all that. I'm done working. I'm retiring. Who cares?"

Taking a cue from Michelle Obama's "when they go low, we go high," I said, "What about your daughter? What about your granddaughter? What about their lives and their future?" No answer.

I'm not advocating for gender equity so my retired family member has a better life. I'm trying to move the needle for her granddaughter and my daughters. This is my life's work. The work of a middle-aged feminist. But Chris and I also have to equip our girls to be their own feminists. What do we teach them?

- Accept who you are.

- Never let others tell you who you are.

- Demand a lot—from yourself and from life.

- Read. Learn. Be curious. Explore.

- Question everything, especially people in authority.

- Be able to provide for yourself and your loved ones.

- Find great people. Surround yourself with them.

- Dream it, achieve it.

- Have faith, hope, and love.

- Make the world a better place for everyone.

partner to find fulfillment in life. I would say that a solid foundation, in whatever form it takes, is as critical as the air we breathe. It's faster and far less complex to launch from steady ground than from constantly shifting sand.

Perhaps it's more telling to state what these women don't have: They don't have a chaotic personal life. They're not Wonder Woman in public and a train wreck in private. They have interests outside work that they embrace and find meaning in. They have loved ones.

And they love their work. They love how they earn a living. They love contributing to the world through skills for which people are willing to pay.

They have a life that makes them happy.

# femtech founder

At 13, Surbhi Sarna began experiencing severe pelvic pain. While ovarian cysts are fairly common for women and often present minimal pain and concern, Surbhi wasn't so lucky. Faced with the choice of going under the knife—and risking infertility—or toughing it out, she chose to wait and hope it would resolve itself. Fortunately, it eventually did.

The experience shaped her life. She studied molecular biology and engineering at UC Berkeley and then worked first as a clinical scientist at Stanford University and later as a research engineer at Abbott and another medical technology company. In 2012, she founded nVision, a medical device company in the underserved women's health sector.

To date, Surbhi (with a dozen medical patents to her name) has raised $17 million in venture capital for the firm, enabling nVision to invent and pursue FDA approval on two much-needed pieces of technology that make detecting ovarian cancer and infertility far easier and more cost effective. When fully brought to market, these two devices will change the lives of millions of women around the world.

*Let's talk about getting VC funding as a woman who started a medical device company for women's health—a largely underfunded area of the market—and in an ecosystem that tends to fund older, white men with a lot of letters after their names.*

So much of my life has been dedicated to women's health. Not only am I a woman trying to do business, but I'm a woman trying to make a women's health opportunity look attractive to male investors in a field that's dominated by men.

But what are the challenges to getting funding? There are a number of confounding factors. I'm in health care, where most folks who start companies have not only a ton of experience but multiple advanced degrees. I don't have a lot of experience running other companies. In fact, my background isn't business at all; I trained as a scientist.

Fortunately, I've had a lot of very supportive mentors and investors, both men and women. When I think about my experience as a woman pitching a women's health-care company, my experience with men has been especially positive.

I don't know if being a woman has given me a leg up or presented me with different setbacks along the way. I think that every entrepreneur is going to have different challenges. The important thing is, even if your path is harder than someone else's, that you still get to whatever goal you were trying to get to.

*You have an especially unique experience in that your husband is also a VC-backed, Silicon Valley-based entrepreneur.*

Yes, Rajeev has raised something like $42 million from some of the top venture funds in the Valley for his startup Reflektive, which now has over a hundred people. Sometimes we do compare and contrast our experiences.

The biggest difference I see is how we develop relationships with investors. He often gets invited to drinks or dinners so that investors can get to know him and his personality. For a lot of reasons, I think male investors are a little more hesitant to do that with a young woman. So one thing I do have to do differently is have more meetings in a more formal structure.

I do know that you really have to know your stuff, especially as a woman entrepreneur. If people have an unconscious bias or even a hidden bias, you have to overcome that with domain expertise and focusing on the investment, so that they're asking, "Do I want to get involved in this area? Is this a good opportunity?"

### *What about being an Indian entrepreneur?*

Silicon Valley has an interesting relationship with those of us with an Indian heritage. A lot of successes have involved Indian men, so I don't know if being Indian is necessarily advantageous, but we're not in quite the same situation many other minorities find themselves in. I can't say that I face anything blatantly discriminatory based on my skin color.

### *The disrupters I know don't get up in the morning thinking,* **How am I going to be discriminated against today?** *That's just not their reality. It sounds like the same is true for you?*

Think about everything that goes into running a company. You can't take on the additional mental burden of wondering, *Is the person I'm about to meet sexist? Racist?* That kind of mentality is a sure way to hold back any minority trying to achieve something. In order to succeed at this game, you have to have enough mind space available to think about the business, leading, innovation, your team—how could you possibly stay competitive if you take on the additional burden of thinking about how hard things are for you or what additional barriers you have to face because you're a woman or have darker skin? All your available time has to go into strategizing, creating an appropriate company culture, attracting investors, and developing products.

Entrepreneurs already have a terrible work-life balance, sky-high divorce rates, sky-high depression and anxiety rates, and that's regardless of gender, identity, and race. You can't add another layer on top of that of worrying about other people's biases.

**You've mentioned company culture and women in the workplace. Do you have a set of policies specifically for your female employees?**

If you take the approach where you say, "Oh, I'm hiring women; I need to have a culture that is more flexible for them," what you're doing long-term is screwing women. You're enabling the shift of responsibilities onto them.

Why should a mother be more responsible for her child than the father? Why should the care of the elderly be placed on the woman's shoulders, and not both? It doesn't matter how flexible your job is if you're expected to take care of your business and take care of your child and take care of your parents.

My husband is a very successful entrepreneur. We had a baby six months ago and we care for my mother. There's no disparity between Rajeev's responsibilities and mine. I think that's where we need to go as a society, not to offer women more flexibility per se, because then as a society we're saying that it's OK that we put more of these responsibilities on women.

What I do in my company is allow flexibility, regardless of if you're a man or a woman. I'm in business; why would I want to make special accommodations for a woman's work schedule but not my male employees? Why would a company ever do that?

*For women who want to work toward gender equity in the workplace, what advice would you give them?*

Remember that you aren't superhuman. Things have to give in certain areas. You can't link your happiness or your sense of fulfillment to the expectation of what you think society sees as success.

People don't have an incentive to call you successful. When you raise funding, people will say, "Oh, well, it probably wasn't that hard to do. All she did was get a check."

Then when you hit a milestone in your company's growth, they'll say, "Oh, well, she'll never reach any kind of serious growth. And you know they're never going to get FDA clearance."

Then when you sell your first company, they're going to say, "Yeah, but it was only for $200 million. What's the big deal?"

Even if you sold your company for a billion dollars, they'd say, "She got lucky. She couldn't do it again."

As long as you link your self-worth to anybody else's expectations, you're just setting yourself up for failure. Forgive me for touching on a darker subject, but you could die tomorrow. Do you want to be in a state where you died trying to get everyone else's approval? Because as long as that's your mindset, that's the place you'll always be in. You can't please everyone; it's never going to happen.

You have to know what's important to you. If I died tomorrow, my family knows I loved them. My employees know that I sincerely cared about them and that I was always doing my best by them. I'll know that I did the things that made me fulfilled. I didn't chase the feeling of trying to be looked up to.

When I was on the Forbes "30 Under 30" list, I constantly had people asking me, "How did you get on that list?" That's such a ridiculous question. Do what you're passionate about, and if you somehow make the list, then great, but being on hte list is not the goal. The goal is not to have recognition by other people. The goal is to satisfy yourself, your own desires, and what you want to achieve. And if that lands you in a place where you have recognition, that's fantastic.

*On one hand, you could frame your story as a woman who had a women's health-care problem and decided to create a women's health-care tech company. On the other, you could frame it as a typical startup founder: a person experienced a problem, realized there was a gap in the marketplace, and created a solution that filled that need.*

You could, and both would be true.

But when I think about my company and our technology, the bigger story is: Did I do what I was put here on this earth to do? On my deathbed, I want to know: Did I make this world a better place for women? Did I enhance women's health? Did I enhance women's place in business?

That's the story I wonder about.

↗  ↗  ↗

What a woman—and barely in her 30s! She accomplished more in her 20s than most people do in a lifetime. Can you imagine what she'll do in the next decade?

I love her attitude about being a woman of color. She just doesn't have the time to think about other people's potential prejudice—she's too busy changing the world.

When she expressed the sentiment that she didn't make allowances for women, I wondered where she was going. Once she finished the thought, though, I saw her point. My question was really more about how she was enabling her women team members vs. having special policies just for women, but she addressed a great point: Changing workplace norms necessitates a change in societal norms. So long as women are expected to be "in charge" of the home, the kids, and their parents, they'll always feel overwhelmed. Surbhi's point is that the more organizations create policies and processes that accommodate these norms, the longer women will find themselves stuck on that hamster wheel. She is saying that nVision won't be party to that.

Coming back to her personal choices, I admire the fact that, unlike the stereotypical "bro culture" traits displayed by so many VC-backed Silicon Valley entrepreneurs, Surbhi isn't driven by ego. She's already past the question "How big can we make this company?"—if she ever had that thought in the first place. She's driven by that same sense of purpose I see as one of the defining traits of disrupters. She knows that regardless of whether her company is worth $200 million or $2 billion, it'll never be enough in some people's eyes. She's defining her success not by someone else's metric, but by her own intrinsic values.

# FOUR

# get out of your head

*"I 'evolved' my ability to be able to talk about myself."*

—Dissertation research participant

once attended a closed-door session at a tech conference. The session's panel included two longtime women's advocates: entrepreneur Vivek Wadhwa and venture capitalist Brad Feld.

In the audience was a husband-and-wife team who had founded the region's most successful digital storytelling company. She served as CEO while he was the head of product development. During the Q&A portion, the husband stood up to pose a question to the panel. Pointing to his wife, he said, "You've got to help our CEO. She can't seem to make a decision fast enough. We run really lean, and we need to make 50 to 60 mission-critical decisions a day—and we're waiting around on her!"

Let's stop and examine everything wrong with this picture.

First, can you imagine an executive in any company pulling that stunt with their CEO? They'd be fired in a heartbeat for embarrassing their chief exec, if nothing else. Now, try to imagine this scene with the genders reversed: him as CEO and her over product development. It just wouldn't happen.

Second, what kind of culture does that signal? If the husband can publicly humiliate his wife at a conference, can you imagine how much of that attitude pervades their workplace with peers, co-workers, and subordinates?

Next, think about the question. He didn't ask the panel for advice on how to make better decisions—just faster ones. Their company was at the forefront in their industry's geography with her at the helm. He never stopped to ask whether her leadership and her lengthy decision-making process had driven those results.

Finally, think about their marriage. I'd kill Chris if he did that to me. I don't know what kind of relationship they had, but I can't imagine that was a comfortable plane ride home. The crazy thing is that I think he was trying to "help" his wife. The problem is that she didn't need help. He did.

When he finished his question (his rant, really), you could have heard a pin drop. You could almost hear people thinking, *Did he really just call out his wife in front of God and everybody?*

I love what happened next, though: One of the panelists (I can't remember which) said, "Shouldn't she be the one standing up? Maybe you and the rest of your team need to learn how to work with her and the way she makes decisions. Because *she's* the CEO. Your job is to make the widgets. Her job is to look at the implications of every decision."

I could have given them a standing ovation.

We still invest in research to justify that qualified women should be in high-profile, high-impact, and high-influence positions. Thank

## My Proudest Comeback to Being Mansplained

Despite being miserably sick, I still had to spend most of the week in an airplane traveling from site to site. You could see from my demeanor that I was obviously not in the best of moods.

You could also obviously see that I am an experienced traveler. Once you have few hundred flights under your belt, you acquire this air of seasoned boredom. It is what it is.

So put yourself in my shoes when I relate the story of what happened to me on this particular flight.

The plane had rolled to the gate. I was in first class together with my fellow business travelers. Everyone had taken off their seatbelts. Those of us in aisle seats had stood. The plane doors had yet to open, so there was nothing to do but wait.

The man who'd sat next to me in the window seat—who had not been good at sharing our arm rest and who had commandeered *my* space under the seat in front me for the rest of *his* bags—suddenly addressed me: "Okay, so look, this is what you need to do," and went on to loudly and obnoxiously tell me the sequence of actions I needed to take in order to optimize deplaning time.

You get used to people sharing their "opinions" and outright rudeness during air travel. It's normal. For the most part, you learn to run with it. This guy, though, was so patronizing and entirely oblivious to the people around him that I decided to interrupt his unconscious bias.

I looked at him for a moment, then said, "Did you just mansplain to me how to get out of your way so you could get off the plane?"

Confused, he said, "What?"

"Did you just mansplain to me how to get out of your way so that you can hurry up and get off the plane?"

His flustered response was drowned out by the women in the cabin cheering and the men chuckling or even outright laughing. After turning a crimson shade—whether from embarrassment, anger, or both, I don't know—he stayed quiet.

I would probably have been a little kinder if I hadn't already felt miserable. Hopefully, though, his embarrassment will save some other woman the tedium of his mansplaining in the future. Not my finest moment; blaming and shaming is not my preferred method of disruption. But sometimes people are so wrapped up in their own world that you have to employ . . . alternative tactics.

goodness we are now seeing a movement that goes beyond "Why do we need more women?" and toward "How do we attract, retain, and develop the women in our talent pool?"

Let me stop here to say that I don't believe women should have all the leadership positions and board seats. I don't believe we do business better than men. That's just sexist.

I do know we approach business differently.

We bring real value to the proverbial table. But is that the message we hear? No. The concept pounded into us from nearly every source is, "You don't have the skills, you don't have the network, you don't have the background, you don't have the right personality, you don't have the requisite experience—you're simply not good enough." That's what women face across the globe. We just don't do it right.

We hear this message so often that we begin to believe it. Imagine if someone told your daughter or sister that they weren't good enough, smart enough, disciplined enough, or talented enough to hold a job. I'd never let someone say that to my girls . . . and yet we say these things to ourselves every day.

*"When the whole world is silent, even one voice becomes powerful."*

—Malala Yousafzai

## We Just Don't Have What It Takes, Do We?

The private equity firm Kleiner Perkins Caufield & Byers (aka Kleiner Perkins) is legendary, having funded such giants as Google, Amazon, AOL, Compaq, and Sun Microsystems—just to name a few. They made headlines in a bad way, though, when junior partner Ellen Pao filed a gender discrimination suit alleging that, among other details, the firm paid men more than their female peers, gave them more opportunities, and allowed female junior partners such as Ellen to sit on only one company board at a time while men could serve on as many as they wanted. The firm, of course, strenuously denied any such discriminatory practices.

This wasn't back in the *Mad Men* era. She filed suit in 2012.

We've been talking about the inherent bias in corporate culture, so I might buy being blind to the wage gap or a subjective issue such as "more opportunities." Even in well-run, well-meaning companies, unconscious discrimination exists. The policy of allowing women to sit on only one board floors me, though.

If you're not familiar with equity firms, sitting on a company board is a big deal because you get ownership equity (i.e., stock). Just imagine if you'd been a board member when Kleiner Perkins funded Google and had stock from the beginning. You'd be set for life. For female partners like Ellen, not being able to sit on multiple boards seriously restricts their potential.

*"Genius is evenly distributed across zip codes. Access and opportunity are not."*

—Mitch Kapor

The underlying assumption of such a policy is that women just don't have what it takes. A man could handle three or four or ten board seats . . . but a woman? She wouldn't have the—what? Stamina? Energy? Focus? Mental capacity?—to handle more than one.

A few months after filing her lawsuit, Ellen was fired, ostensibly for her performance; she wasn't a "team player." She joined Reddit, eventually becoming CEO. Prior to resigning from Reddit, one of her hallmark policies there was banning revenge porn (where exes—usually the boyfriend—post private pictures of their partner online after breaking up).

I won't demonize Kleiner Perkins, nor will I canonize Ellen. But do I believe that an old money boys' club afforded women the same opportunities available to their male partners? Don't make me laugh.

Mary Spio founded CEEK VR, a virtual reality platform with clients such as Universal, Warren Buffett's Berkshire Hathaway, Lucasfilm, Fox, and Microsoft. Mary herself is an electrical engineer whose employment history includes working as a deep space engineer (badass, right?) and running Boeing's satellite communication systems. With such a stellar resume, you'd imagine that venture capitalists would be begging to fund her already-successful startup. Nope. The last time we spoke, she was struggling to understand what she was or wasn't doing that kept her from landing the capital she needed.

As amazing as she is, even she was made to doubt herself.

Yes, there are injustices and double standards in business. The heroines I've interviewed or worked with acknowledge that the cards are stacked against them. There is a bias against women across the board. But instead of complaining about it, they find ways to circumvent or overcome those challenges. The question is, how do we handle it?

To quote from my dissertation:

> ". . . although obstacles may exist, the inaction to overcome
> the obstacles or acceptance that barriers impeded success were
> self-imposed and avoidable."

In other words, my research found that, like Dorothy wearing her ruby slippers, they had the power to get where they wanted to go all along. All they needed was someone to help them understand how to use what they already possessed.

*"On ne naît pas femme: on le devient."*
*("One is not born, but rather becomes, a woman.")*

—Simone de Beauvoir, *Le Deuxième Sexe*

## Getting Rid of Doubt, Inside and Out

Women's mentoring programs, training programs, leadership programs, and the like place the onus on us. We'd have better salaries if we'd just copy what our male counterparts are doing. Never mind that, across the board, women with the same education, experience, and responsibilities still don't earn what men do. It's not an HR compensation problem. It's not the system. It's us.

Yeah, right.

The default reaction is to internalize these messages. Women begin to feel that they're not good enough. Something's wrong with them. If only they were better. If only they had gone to this school or knew those people. If only they weren't a woman.

I am here to say that it's not us. It's the system. Our job is to understand the system and navigate around it or use it to harness all talent, including our own. And, in the process, we change the system.

Forgive me if this is a clichéd analogy, but think of Helen Keller. Rendered blind and deaf after a childhood illness, she faced incredible—some would even say insurmountable—adversity. She knew she couldn't live the life of her seeing and hearing peers. But instead of giving up in frustration, she—with help—overcame those challenges and became an accomplished woman, writing books and touring the world.

The women I showcase in this book face an analogous challenge. They can't win the game playing with their handicap (i.e., competing

## 13 Cold but Common Things We Say to Ourselves

1. You're the problem.

2. You're not good enough.

3. You're a fraud.

4. You don't belong here.

5. Someone else could do it better.

6. Everyone else knows what's going on.

7. The cards are stacked against you—you'll never win.

8. Better to sit here and look dumb than open your mouth and remove all doubt.

9. They all laugh at you.

10. You're not a good mother. You're not a good daughter. You're not a good wife. You're not a good friend.

11. You'll never make it.

12. Better quit while you're ahead.

13. You're going to fail.

as a woman in a culture of masculinity). So they find ways to compete wherein they can win. It was a skill they had to learn, though.

I want to show you specific examples of how they did so, but the more important lesson I learned from these women is their mindset. Instead of internalizing this barrage of self-doubt aimed at them, they saw it for what it was: the skewed perspective of a culture biased against their gender. They neutralized these messages.

They didn't let it get to them.

Take Stephanie Buscemi, an executive vice president at Salesforce, a brilliant woman, and one of my professional heroines. Stephanie oozes integrity and confidence—an earned executive presence thanks to a highly successful career in enterprise technology. Very early in career, she attended a strategy meeting on customer acquisition where a very senior male executive asked her, "Do you promise to wear that pink sweater to the meeting? That will close the deal!" She said, "I had a choice, Patti. I could be the victim and let him undermine my influence. Or I could neutralize the comment and call him out on it."

## Brené Brown and "The Power of Vulnerability"

Have you seen Brené Brown's TED Talk? It's one of the ten most-viewed TED Talks in the world.

Why, though? Why does a 20-minute talk about shame, emotional breakdown, and self-help-esque revelations continue to be one of the most-watched videos of the entire TED Talk series?

I mean, at one point this video vied for top popularity against the likes of Steve Jobs ("How to live before you die"), Stephen Hawking ("Questioning the universe"), Elizabeth Gilbert ("Your elusive creative genius"), Daniel Pink ("The puzzle of motivation"), Barry Schwartz ("The paradox of choice"), and—of course—Mary Roach's "Ten things you didn't know about orgasms."

Why does a video about shame and opening ourselves up keep drawing people in? I believe it's what Brené speaks to: We want to be vulnerable. We struggle with being vulnerable. It's exposing. Being vulnerable is akin to being weak. Yet, in true cognitive dissonance, we want to be our authentic selves. We want to share the burden of our inner selves with others.

We long to belong.

She took the second path. After the meeting, she approached her peers and superiors one-on-one and called attention to the real problem. Once she pointed out the absurdity of him focusing on her physical appearance, they agreed with her and rallied behind her. In the end, he looked foolish and lost the respect of his peers. Stephanie showed courage in being a subordinate and yet speaking up.

## Finding Confidence Despite the Criticism

I wish I could say these disrupters let sexist critiques flow off them like water off a duck's back, but it takes time to learn—or, rather, unlearn—how to stop internalizing criticism and begin to neutralize it.

It takes practice to shift from "Everybody says I need to change how I do things . . . maybe they're right?" to "Let's focus on what's important here, and ignore what isn't." The women I interviewed are amazingly good at this. Even if there's an old white dude threatened by the only woman in the room and he's coming after her with a vengeance, a disrupter is adept at placing his attack in context and not letting it derail her from her goals.

> **"**Take criticism seriously, but not personally. If there
> is truth or merit in the criticism, try to learn from it.
> Otherwise, let it roll right off you.**"**
>
> —Hillary Clinton

One of my interviewees told me, "There aren't a lot of women who have the confidence and self-esteem to fit in what is, quite honestly, always a group of men. I'm the only woman, always. The key to my success has been to add my points without feeling intimidated."

Another described her "painful experience of feeling stupid without being willing to believe it." It used to be that when she had a question, she automatically assumed the problem was with her. Now, through experience and developing her confidence, "when there's a problem, the answer isn't that I'm dumb. That was a huge step for me."

From the time we're little girls, women spend a lifetime exposed to the constant barrage of negativity that we need more skills vis-à-vis men. We're traditionally raised to expect to do different work than men. Even though it's a half-century out of date, much of the U.S. still holds on to that 1950s image of the husband going to work while June Cleaver stays home to manage the household. During that era, it was mostly true: in about 70 percent of households, daddy went to work and mommy stayed home. Of course, that's been the traditional role for millennia: the men left the cave while the women reared the kids. And if you're a caveman, there's a certain logic in letting the stronger of the species go risk their lives wrestling woolly mammoths while those with the mammary glands nurse the young.

But we're not cavemen anymore. The 1950s is more than a half-century behind us. Returning to that study we presented in the last chapter, today, not only is it normal to have dual-earning families (60 percent in the U.S.[1]), but we've even seen a surge of maternal breadwinners (40 percent of U.S. households and almost a third of European[2]) where the mother earns at least half the family income—if not all.[3] Of these, many are headed by single mothers: almost two-thirds of the maternal breadwinners in the U.S.,[4] for example, and about half in both the U.K. and Germany.[5]

> "Creativity is God's gift to us. Using our creativity is our gift back to God."
>
> —Julia Cameron

Despite these demographic trends, we're still expected to fulfill the traditional role of a woman: More than half the survey respondents in the Pew Research Center's 2013 "Breadwinner Moms"[6] study said that children are better off if the mother doesn't work outside the home; just 8 percent said the same about the father. We spend a lifetime exposed to the constant barrage of negativity. We're made to live by a certain set of expectations that don't exist for men. It's normal for a man to be a gynecologist, but it's novel for a woman to be a proctologist. Girls are still channeled into traditionally feminine roles and careers. We're forced to play a rigged game where, even if we follow the rules, we lose.

Instead of neutralizing these messages, we internalize them. It becomes a personal attack (instead of recognizing it for the systemic bias it is). From entry-level employee to CEO to board member, women are constantly bombarded with the message—implicitly or, in the case of the husband at the tech conference, publicly—that we aren't enough. We need to be something else. We need to change. We need to be "more."

> **"***I look back at the year when I started to act more like myself and less like many of the men around me. That was the turning point for me in my career. I would never be on the boards I'm on today if I hadn't made that change.***"**
>
> —Dissertation research participant

What breaks my heart is listening to women who have internalized that message. Despite impressive accomplishments, newsworthy achievements, selfless sacrifice for loved ones, and overcoming incredible odds, their internal monologues match what they've been fed their whole lives.

They've been made to feel "less" to the point that they believe it.

It's not really about overconfidence or a lack of confidence, though. It's about believing in yourself despite your self-doubt (triggered from within and without). It's about the painful experience of feeling stupid even when you don't believe it. It's relying on your past experiences, on your demonstrated ability to rise to the challenge, and on your capacity to do so again.

## Stop Listening to "Act More Like a Man"

In the early days of my career, I kept getting invited to events for women: networking, training, "development opportunities," and the like. At every one of them, the message was, "Look at these men. Look at how successful they are. Look at how much better their salaries are. That's because they're great at negotiating and networking, and you suck. Learn how to negotiate like a man."

It's not that your human resources department lacks a compensation strategy to ensure equal pay for equal work. It's not that your company lacks inclusion practices. No, it's you. There's something wrong with you. If only you were more like a man. If only you tried harder.

It's always about fixing women . . . but you don't need fixing.

# a fully formed woman— finally!

The other interviews I've presented in *Disrupters* have been focused on a theme or a line of thinking. Here, I wanted to present something longer—something deeper. Hence, this is more of a life journey than a discussion.

I wanted to tell you the story of Lisa Morales-Hellebo because of how many times it's the story of "Well, that didn't work. What now?" It's the journey of a disrupter who, I suspect, is just now coming into her own. It's your chance to see the midpoint of someone on her way to disrupting an entire industry.

Also, I want it on record that "I knew her when . . ."

Instead of displaying her impressive experience upfront, I'm not going to bias you. I want you to see how those accomplishments came about. That is, I want you to see the process instead of just the result.

### Lisa, let's start at the beginning.

I'm a first-generation Puerto Rican, born here and raised in the Bronx. When I was about three, my father wanted better opportunities for my siblings and me, so we moved to Westchester, New York.

If you've never been to Westchester, it is extremely wealthy and extremely white. It's where Martha Stewart and the Clintons live. Moving there from the Bronx did give us better opportunities, but it had its ugly side, too.

We were the only brown family in our town for quite a while. As fate would have it, we lived two doors down from a super racist, hate-filled man. He would dump bloody, severed deer heads in our driveway; he'd write "spic" in the snow outside our house; he'd cross the street if he saw us walking his way; he'd beat his children if they waved hello to us. I remember as young as 5 years old realizing that if I were playing at the neighbor's house and his child came over there to play, too, that I needed to leave so he wouldn't get beaten for playing with me. And it wasn't just him. On the school bus, we were called "spic" and "n—." Kids would spit on me to "give me a shower" because my skin was so "dirty."

My escape was drawing. I loved doing creative things. Around 8 years of age, I'd ask my mom to get *Vogue* and *Bazaar* or any fashion magazine, which quickly became my world. I fell absolutely in love with fashion and the supermodels of the '80s. I loved the idea that you could become a whole other person just by changing your clothes, makeup, and hair—that you could become something bigger than you were. My play became cutting up magazines and redoing the layouts, having no idea I'd become a graphic designer someday. All I knew was that I wanted to work for *Vogue*.

The only college I applied to was Carnegie Mellon. I didn't want to go to Parsons, Rhode Island School of Design, or universities like them because they were purely fine arts schools. I applied to Carnegie Mellon's design school because it was highly prestigious and provided a balanced curriculum. I wasn't quite sure what design was, but I knew that I wanted to do something creative that made real money.

Thank goodness Carnegie Mellon accepted me because I had no backup plan. My parents tried to talk me into going to Syracuse University. "Are you sure, Lisa? They're giving you a full ride and everything after just your portfolio review!" Nope. It was Carnegie Mellon or bust.

Their design school was way ahead of the design thinking movement. I tell people that I got a design thinking degree. I learned how to apply design thinking methodologies, which really enabled my career and has even become a sought-after business skill set.

### And that's how you got into the fashion industry?

Actually, I was interviewing for my dream job at *Vogue* when a professor called me. He said, "Lisa, can you get out to Michigan tomorrow? I recommended you for an internship at Herman Miller. They have 4,500 applicants a year, and they only have two slots. I told them you're my top pick, and they want you to fly out tomorrow."

I didn't go directly into fashion: I went to work at a world-renowned furniture company in Michigan. It was an amazing experience that allowed me to expand my design vocabulary while working with world-renowned designers. I got to see that design is truly a process—it's not art. I was there while they were developing the Aeron chair, and let me tell you: Some of the initial concepts weren't pretty.

But I hated Michigan. Hell is not hot. It's a freezing-cold place somewhere in the middle of a Michigan winter. I said, "I am never going to live in a place this cold again," and got my Puerto Rican butt out of there.

*OK, so design school and then Herman Miller . . . then fashion?*

Sort of.

I worked at a number of different marketing agencies and wound up working with a small in-house firm—literally. It was in his house. He'd been in business for seven years, but he still ran everything out of a home office.

One day, I said, "OK, it's just you and me, but I can't stand the clutter and lack of process. Can I just organize everything?"

He said, "Sure!" and handed me his credit card. And that is how I learned how to run an agency. I was barely two years out of college, managing huge accounts for Kathy Ireland and Blue Cross Blue Shield.

I learned so much, for which I'm grateful, but I knew I wanted to dive more into this web thing. There was an agency in Boston that had done the LAX signage and the World Cup's environmental graphics and had just started building a web arm. They wanted me to be one of the three pillars of their new division. So I moved to Boston and got ready to start my job when the two other new hires had a huge fight with the boss and quit, which meant they scrapped the whole idea.

So there I was, in Boston, with no friends and no job.

I took a job at a small agency that did about 80 percent print work. Within a year, I grew their web development so that about 80 percent of the company's revenue came from web. We finally broke a million dollars in revenue for the first time in the agency's history—and I was still the only web person.

I said, "Can I have a raise?" No. "Well, then, can I hire some people?" No. "Well, then, buh-bye."

At the same time, I'd fallen in love with data and saw that companies' content-management software was becoming the next big thing. I found work with a content-management startup in DC. By "startup," I mean I was hire number 20. As the design manager, my job was to land big-name clientele for website redesign projects where we would implement our content-management software.

I was pitching against giants like Razorfish, Sapient, and iXL. Within a year, we landed about 30 big accounts, like NASCAR and *George* magazine. This was back in the heyday of the dotcom era, where the employee of the month got to drive the company's BMW Z3 convertible. It was crazy. Within a year, we were acquired, and the CEO asked me to stay on as the chief marketing officer, but being CMO of a big content-management software company didn't appeal to me. I was looking for something different.

***Diving off head-first into something—whether by choice or necessity—doesn't look like it bothers you.***

I didn't realize at the time that I was really an entrepreneur at heart. I like seeing companies grow, I like creating something from nothing, and I like doing the impossible.

***Moving to a tech startup scene like Silicon Valley must have been heaven.***

You know, you'd think so, but I somehow missed the memo that the dotcom bubble was just about to burst. The big consultancy iXL, who'd been one of our competitors, offered me a job. Four months after I'd settled in, the firm went bust. The bubble had popped.

There I found myself, with zero contacts and zero network, in a city where you could spit out your window and hit a dozen graphic designers and creative directors like me.

***Oh, God—it was Boston all over again.***

Story of my life, right?

I found out about a tech job fair going on in San Francisco. I said, "You know, I've never believed the rules applied to me. No, I'm not a techie. Yes, I know some HTML and PHP, but you wouldn't hire me to build a whole platform. But I don't care. I'm going to go talk myself into a job."

And I did. I came across a company called Ubiquity, founded by the same guy who founded the children's toy tech company LeapFrog, Jim Marggraff. They brought me in to meet Jim, and the two of us talked for hours. The whole team said, "Look, we don't know what to do with you or how you fit here, but we need you." Hired.

I was creative director for all of two-and-a-half weeks before the parent company decided to withdraw all funding because the whole tech world was imploding all around us. They told us, "Come by and pick up your final checks tomorrow. Buh-bye."

### I can see the movie now: "The Yo-Yo Life of Lisa Morales."

Right? It was just one roller coaster after another.

I went through some job placement sites, a few headhunters, and a lot of crappy interviews. Then a friend who'd been at iXL called me and wanted me to come work with him at the new company he'd landed at.

"What do they do?" I asked.

"Online customized cosmetics."

My head exploded: I had to work there.

The company was owned by Procter & Gamble, the global consumer goods company, and backed by a huge venture capital fund in Silicon Valley. It sounded perfect.

I interviewed for the job, my friend vouched for me, and I got hired on as his art director for the website. Immediately, I started sticking my nose where it didn't belong. I told them that spending $30,000 to retouch a photograph that was only going to be used online was insane. I mean, burning through money was something that didn't happen in the scrappy spots I always found myself in. I convinced them to let me spend $5,000 on a camera and some setup, and we started shooting everything in-house.

I kept finding ways to add value, create efficiencies, and question why things were done the way they were. I pissed a lot of people off, but I delivered results and the CEO loved it, so I kept going.

Inside a month, I had re-architected the skin-care line. Literally, nothing existed until you had created it on the website. You went through a series of questions and got to customize your own cosmetics. I felt like I was playing.

About a month after redesigning the customer experience for that line, skin-care sales tripled. The company fired my boss and gave me his job. A few months after that, I was promoted to creative director for the entire company and got to present to the board, including Geoff Yang from Redpoint Ventures and A.G. Lafley, the chairman, president, and CEO of Procter & Gamble. When A.G. shook my hand and congratulated me on re-creating the company's brand, I am fairly certain the clouds parted and angels sang. This was a dream job.

Yet again, for me, it just felt like I was having fun. Getting to create algorithms and graphics, playing with code, coming up with the whole customer experience. I loved it.

I had another idea: We shouldn't use supermodels—we needed to use real women to sell our cosmetics. I said, "If you want personalized cosmetics, you want to see it on a person you identify with. I don't look like a supermodel—I don't relate to a supermodel. I relate to everyday women. I need to know that somebody real is getting behind these products. That's the strongest form of marketing."

I proposed something radical at the time (back in 2000): Photograph the women in our office.

The folks from P&G jokingly said, "Ahhh . . . all you ladies in our office are hideous. That's what you want to use in your marketing?"

I fought, and they finally said, "OK, you can try your little idea out on our Yahoo! banner ads." You know, those little banners at the top of the page that we all ignore these days?

We did, and they became the highest clickthrough banners for all of Yahoo! that year. Keep in mind, this was in the heyday of Yahoo!, so this was a pretty big deal. Yahoo! brought me down to their headquarters to do a video for their marketing team about peer-to-peer marketing and social recommendations, long before the dawn of Facebook, Instagram, or Twitter.

My job was amazing. I felt like it was the grown-up version of me sitting around with cutouts of *Vogue* magazines, mixing and matching things together to see what worked and what looked good. I was in heaven.

**So if the story of your life holds true, this should be about the time that everything falls apart. Again.**

Yes, but in a good way!

I met this tall, blond, green-eyed, Viking surfer of a man who became my husband. It was like something out of a movie: He walked up to my friend, asked her to introduce us, and two hours later strangers were asking us how long we'd been together.

Fast-forward through getting married in Spain and living in his native Norway for three years. We wanted to have kids, so we decided to come back stateside. I moved to DC and looked for a job that would be stable enough to let him quit his and join me.

I convinced the CEO of a big retail chain based in DC to hire me—and he took some convincing. At first, he barely wanted to do anything via multichannel promotions. Then when he started seeing results, we dialed it up. We made a mark for ourselves when we got ahead of a Tempur-Pedic promotion. We were their only retailer who did a true omnichannel campaign. We blew the lid off it: We had the highest single-distributor sales month in the history of Tempur-Pedic.

It was like Yahoo! again: The CEO flew me to their headquarters to talk to their marketing team, and then wanted me to fly the next morning to another regional headquarters.

At that point, I was an obvious seven months along in my first pregnancy. I pointed to my stomach and said, "Do you see that I have a human growing inside me?"

He said, "I know, we need you more than you need us. I assume you're going to start your own company or something when you go out on maternity leave. Would you like your first client?"

And that's how I became an entrepreneur.

*Can we stop right here so I can say how impressive your resilience is? It's like no matter how high or how low you find yourself, you just keep moving forward. "Oh, that worked. Cool." "Oh, that failed. Crap."*

Oh, I've had to pick myself up off the floor more times than I can count. But just lying there has never been an option. It's just not in my DNA. I have to be doing something that feels challenging.

*OK, so you had your baby and then had your baby.*

It was crazy. As soon as I went out on maternity leave, I had people from all these companies I'd worked at say, "Hey, we just found out you went on maternity leave. Are you going to start an agency? Can we hire you?"

I said, "Guys, I just made a human. Can you give me a couple of months?"

In two years, my little company I ran out of the basement of my house in the suburbs of DC was an agency of record for Coca-Cola and some other great clients. I grossed more than $400,000 working nine-to-five, with no evenings or weekends. I trained my clients so well, I'd be on the phone with the guys at Coca-Cola and they'd say, "Oh, it's 4:50 p.m. We'd better get off the phone so you can go get your babies. We'll pick this up in the morning!" I knew that mutual respect was earned through my consistent results and was grateful to work with people who appreciated my design thinking.

*So, if everything was going great, this would be about the time you'd be getting bored. Am I right?*

Yes. The curse of the entrepreneur.

I'd helped a friend do all the marketing for a nonprofit that brings together the top 1 percent of minority wealth in the country. I walked into this ballroom full of black, brown, and Asian millionaires and billionaires. It was one of the most eye-opening experiences of my life.

When I got to talking to them, I found that they really weren't that different. One was even a Puerto Rican from the Bronx! They challenged me: "Yes, you create beautiful images, but what else are you contributing to the world?"

I was like, *Shit, these people are really expecting me to do something!*

From that day forward, my little agency was no longer enough for me.

I started casting about and went to a tech conference in DC where Razorfish and other big guys were onstage talking about Facebook and Twitter being the future of commerce. I said, "No, I don't think so. I think they're great enablers and they can redefine customer service, but I don't think they'll replace shopping. I think the future is a universal shopping platform where brands are agnostic and the experience is about matching my personal preferences, price points, and measurements, and having the data align brands and products with what I want."

The founder of Razorfish said, "That will never happen."

Well, that's the wrong thing to say to someone like me. We'll do it just to prove you wrong. So I did.

It took an incredible amount of work and a hell of a lot of data crunching, but here's the payoff: I went onstage at the DC tech meetup in front of about a thousand people. We were still working on the code literally five minutes before I went onstage.

I pulled up the website and began by selecting a $4,500 outfit—shoes, handbag, dress, some accessories. Then I selected "items under $100." In two seconds, the platform came back with an identical outfit for $300 compiled from different brands and retailers.

I've never experienced anything like this: I heard a roomful of a thousand people collectively gasp. It was amazing.

I said, "Well, crap. I guess I need to start a company."

### *Finally! You're in the fashion industry!*

Yes. I started a fashion tech company. In the process, I got pulled into a tech accelerator called Techstars. I was hoping it could help me form relationships with the fashion brands and C-level execs at big retailers.

But after months and months of trying to sell to big brands and retailers while raising capital, I decided to try to sell outright before pulling the plug. People either didn't get contextual search or they didn't want to build an entire data department inside their company from the ground up to be able to integrate our tech. We ran out of our cash runway while trying to get to the right decision-makers within a B2B sales cycle, so I finally called it and pulled the plug.

I dissolved the company, and once it was legally shut down, I took down the website.

Literally the next day, I got emails and calls from ASOS, Heels.com, and other big e-tailers saying, "What happened? You've created something we've never seen before: personalized merchandising to the customer of one!"

I was like, "I know. I've been trying to get to you guys."

But instead of going into a founder's depression—which was quite tempting—I said, "This is a problem. We need a fashion tech accelerator that connects the big brands and retailers with the startups looking to serve them. I'm going to build one."

I pitched the idea to Amy Millman at Springboard Enterprises and Kay Koplovitz, the CEO there as well as a board member at Kate Spade and the founder of USA Networks.

They got Kate Spade and J. Crew onboard, then said, "Go!" I had to line up at least ten retailers . . . and launch the website . . . and secure co-working space . . . and get all the legal in order . . . and build our startup applicant pipeline . . . and do the media outreach. I worked 16-hour days for four months.

As soon as we hit the switch on the New York Fashion Tech Lab, the press came fast and furious. Everyone from

*Women's Wear Daily* to *Fast Company* was contacting me. I was just amazed that I had pulled it off with so little lead time or resources.

I stayed through until the first cohort had graduated and I was satisfied that the accelerator was successful. Something like this would have been so helpful when I had my contextual search company. I'm just grateful I got to be part of a change I thought was necessary in the industry.

### Where did your entrepreneurial spirit take you next?

I started looking at the larger ecosystem of fashion and realized nobody was focusing on innovation in the supply chain. Apparel manufacturing is going to become more and more localized, to the point of becoming the point-of-sale. Customization, personalization, and on-demand production— that's where we're going as an industry.

In looking at the supply chain, I had the good fortune to be invited to be on the founding board of Parallel18, Puerto Rico's first-ever startup accelerator. In understanding the excruciating economic crisis the island has been going through, I asked, "How can we leverage this accelerator program to better provide access to the successful companies already on the island?"

My colleagues there said, "We weren't really brought on to do that but if you want to do that, we're happy to help you."

Over the course of a week every month for six months, I went all over Puerto Rico, meeting with manufacturers, maker labs, universities, fashion designers, and anyone else I could speak to. The potential is incredible for small-batch, quick-turnaround, high-quality, ready-to-wear apparel. The infrastructure is there. You have factories sitting idle all over the island. You have out-of-work seamstresses who would jump at the chance to have another manufacturing job. Puerto Rico has the advantage of already being part of the U.S., but enjoys special tax advantages from being a U.S. territory. The

Puerto Rican government has huge subsidies and tax incentives specifically for the textile and apparel manufacturing industry. It's like the fashion industry has a unicorn just a plane ride away from NYC, the fashion epicenter of the world . . . and it has no clue.

But one thing I learned from starting the New York Fashion Tech Lab is that these tech accelerators aren't going to change the core DNA of the fashion industry. Big brands and retailers continue to do business the same way they have for years, despite the fact that the industry is going through the same massive rebirth as other industries.

Right now, I feel like I am playing a game of chess, with all the people, experiences, and insights I've gained. I'm working on redefining the way the fashion and retail industry gains access to innovation, validates it, invests in it, and can create the agility required for innovation. I have a unique background in tech, fashion, art, design, and business, along with an insatiable curiosity. I want to use that to make my dent in the universe.

*Earlier, you said there have been times you had to pick yourself up off the floor. Do you mind talking about that a little more?*

Getting into Techstars was a transformation for me. Less than 1 percent of all companies that apply are accepted. Their alumni have raised billions of dollars in funding, and their incubators are all over the world.

Being accepted was validation for my career—for my whole life, really. I mean, our first night out, I realized that I was among literally rocket scientists. And here I am, this suburban housewife in her basement tinkering with data and code.

The managing director at the incubator in Boston happened to be a woman who seemed to cut into me a lot. I shrugged it off, but a lot of the other male founders were like, "Damn—why is she like that to you? Why is she always digging into you?"

I stayed late one night to talk to her. She told me, "You know, you're pretty mediocre. I'd say you're middle of the pack. Maybe you're a great product person, but perhaps you're just not cut out to be CEO."

I admit it: I went home and bawled my eyes out. I called my mother crying. Somewhere in my conversation with my mom, I finally stopped repressing all this awful stuff that happened to me growing up that I told you about earlier. I had a near total PTSD breakdown.

After I got through my anxiety and the associated panic attack, I went back to the managing director and shared all the awful things that were flooding back into my memory. I opened my heart to this woman. Do you know what she told me?

"We all have baggage. Get over it."

There is only one reason to be that harsh: to gain a power position—not to help the other person in the conversation. Considering the high-stakes world of being a founder, it's no wonder that so many entrepreneurs feel isolated and suffer from depression.

Patti, founders are inherently more prone to anxiety, depression, bipolar disorder, and those kinds of things. It's part of the magic that gives us the ability to see the world differently, but it also makes us more vulnerable in certain ways. Thank God I'm a fully formed human being, because if I weren't, she could have sent me over the edge.

But why? Why did I allow this woman to hold so much power over me? In dealing with all my childhood stuff, I realized that my internal mantra had been "prove your worth."

My entire life, from being in school to tackling challenges to being stubborn enough to prove the founder of Razorfish wrong . . . it had all been about me proving my worth.

That's not me anymore. This has been my year of learning to just not give a fuck.

It's taken me a long time to realize that my whole life has

been a culmination of experiences to prepare me for what I've been put on this planet to do: to reinvent this industry that gave me an escape from the hatred I lived with as a child, and that has informed my life and transformed me into the person I am today.

I'm here to share what I know with the world. Who are you to judge whether I'm worthy? Who are you to define who I am and what I can do?

This is my path, and I'm confident in where I'm headed.

↗ ↗ ↗

One of the many things I love about entrepreneurs, especially female entrepreneurs, is that they are a special breed of crazy. Maybe that's why I have become such a big fan of Lisa. Her life has been spent contradicting social and business systems designed for someone else.

The odds are truly against women founders. On top of that, being an entrepreneur, by its very definition, means always doing something for the first time.

Yet every time, Lisa gets up after failing, dusts herself off, and climbs to even greater heights. Those of us in the startup ecosystem or the tech industry as a whole have a love affair with failure. My business friends in the Silicon Valley wear failure like a badge of honor. It's certainly part of the learning process toward success, but if you are going it alone or don't have the right support, the stress can be debilitating.

The best route to combat the stress of failure is to create an environment where you and the people around you can be both vulnerable and strong, like Lisa, where you can turn the destructive internalization of failure into objective learning.

*Postscript: shortly after our interview, Hurricane Maria devastated Puerto Rico. I wanted to update Lisa's story on her involvement in the recovery just as this book was going to press.*

Yes, Hurricane Maria devastated the island, but the government response has created a humanitarian crisis. People are literally burying their loved ones in their backyards because their villages are still inaccessible months after the hurricane.

Worse, the message isn't getting out. We aren't seeing the media coverage we need, so people are unaware of the extent of the problems and forgetting about it as more time passes.

We—the Puerto Rican diaspora—are tackling the problem from two angles. One is immediate relief. People like my friend Christine Enid Nieves Rodriguez, an Oxford alum and former Entrepreneur in Residence at Florida State, worked to create a communal kitchen in her grandmother's village of that feeds 500 people a day, 5 days a week. Babson College alum Gustavo Diaz pivoted his just-launched entrepreneur housing venture into a recovery planning headquarters. He was ahead of FEMA in driving across the island, speaking to every local mayor, documenting needs, and facilitating and communicating aid.

The second angle is to communicate the long-term needs. Christine is an amazingly talented writer chronicling people's experiences there with hope, grace, and heartbreaking humanity. On my part, I'm working with resources both on and off the island to create content showcasing these stories, humanizing our fellow Americans on the island, and stressing the need for collaboration on sustainable infrastructure. Elon Musk is a great example. He doesn't want to come to Puerto Rico to do a PR piece for his company. He genuinely wants to effect long-term change, but we need a plan for the rebuilding of infrastructure and a sustainable local economy.

We can't wait for "the people in charge" to save Puerto Rico, so we're doing it ourselves.

# use what you've got (everyone else does)

*"Diversity is important, but we can't lower the bar."*

—Twitter senior vice-president

W hy don't employees place a higher priority on diversity?

In part, it's because they don't understand what diversity means. Fifty-three percent of men surveyed for McKinsey & Co.'s 2016 "Women in the Workplace"[1] report say "gender diversity" means to deemphasize individual performance, while 44 percent of the same group believes it means outright favoritism.

Those beliefs lead to statements like "You know, you only got that job because you're a woman." Ever hear that one? I've never had it said to my face, but I've spoken to plenty of women who have. They often feel the unspoken implication is " . . . and don't you forget it." In other words, they got a job they didn't deserve. They had a door opened for them because they were wearing a skirt.

> **"You cannot wait for others to pave the way. You overwhelm prejudice and discrimination with excellence and effort."**
>
> —Ernesta Procope

So what?

There are plenty of people who got a job only because they were:

- the CEO's son
- the chairman's golfing buddy
- a young man with an engineering degree
- a major client's brother-in-law
- a roommate at Yale, Harvard, Wharton, or Stanford
- experienced with Sarbanes-Oxley
- charming

The truth of it is that men are hired for what they might be able to do. Women are hired only if they have proven themselves over and over again. I *wish* we lived in a world where advancement and accomplishment were solely based on merit or potential. I wouldn't need to write this book. We could move past conversations about gender, equity, and access and focus on doing our jobs. We would finally live in Martin Luther King Jr.'s world, where everyone would "not be judged by the color of their skin, but by the content of their character."

Yeah, we're not there yet.

There are a million factors that go into any business decision, both explicit and subconscious. Landing a contract, an invitation, a promotion, or a seat on the board is almost never strictly about the person's qualifications. Yes, sometimes a woman might land a job because she's a woman.

Again: so what?

What if you got a job partly because of a quota system, an HR diversity initiative, or simply so the board could have a token woman? What are you supposed to do? Be glad you get to sit at the grown-ups' table? Not speak up? Not make waves? Be grateful and look pretty while those who "deserve" to be there have all the fun?

No thank you. The women I hold up as examples here don't allow their gender to be a handicap; they see it as a strength. They accept that it may have been a factor in getting them where they are, but they double down and work hard to add real value.

They don't internalize the message that they "only" got the job because they were a woman. They neutralize those messages and look toward the future. They say, "OK, now that I'm here, what can we do to achieve the mission going forward?"

> **"**Sure [Fred Astaire] was great, but don't forget that Ginger Rogers did everything he did . . . backwards and in high heels.**"**
>
> —Bob Thaves

## We Don't Need a Handout

As a wonder woman once told me, "No one's going to get asked to join a board because they're a woman. They'll get asked because they're a *competent* woman who has done something." That sums up the role models we're talking about here. They didn't get where they are because someone did them a favor. They're not just a pretty face. They are impressive women with unique skills, diverse backgrounds, and relevant expertise.

The women in my doctoral research were no exception. One was a CEO scientist with a Ph.D. who could slice and dice data and was used to working with the mind-boggling numbers that come with financing multinational corporations. Another was an

SEC expert with an intimate knowledge of Sarbanes-Oxley, who had numerous mergers and acquisitions deals under her belt. Another had experience working with legislatures at both the state and federal levels. One was the president of two industry trade associations. Another had a background in manufacturing as well as business development.

I could go on and on, but suffice it to say these women weren't handed their board seats just because they were women, and they weren't asking for a handout. They had ambition, vision, domain knowledge, and insight.

In fact, one of them told me, "I'm careful when someone calls me up and says, 'We want to talk to you because you're a woman.' I'm not saying I wouldn't take the interview, but I sure don't want to be the person who has nothing to add—that they only brought me on because I was a woman."

These women have earned the right to be where they are.

## He Only Got That Job Because He's Tall and Handsome

In *Blink*, Malcolm Gladwell points out that less than 4 percent of men in the U.S. are 6 feet 2 inches or taller. Among Fortune 500 CEOs, though, they compose an astounding 30 percent. In short, if you're short, your chances of becoming the chief executive are long odds. (Couldn't resist.) Other studies have pointed out that typical CEOs have a deeper voice than average; have a head of thick, lustrous hair; and are physically fit.[2]

You know what I'd love to tell those CEOs? "Don't forget: You only got this job because you're tall and good-looking." They didn't land their position strictly on merit, education, experience, and potential. Their physical traits played a role.

So . . . they're supposed to just shut up and look pretty, right?

No, of course not. And neither do our rule-breaking heroines. They know we don't live in a corporate culture that bases promotions and opportunities strictly on merit. They accept the fact that they may have gotten a seat on the board because the directors have set an explicit quota, because the company wants good PR, or because they live in quota-mandating Norway.

> **"Whatever women do they must do twice as well as men to be thought half as good."**
>
> —Charlotte Whitton

Engineer Leslie Miley made national headlines in 2015 when he publicly stated his reason for leaving Twitter, forsaking a severance package so he could speak out. He pointed not only to a lack of diversity but an utter lack of commitment to it, as the SVP's quote we opened this chapter with alludes to.

Over one-fourth of all black internet users in the U.S. are on Twitter. With so many such a diverse customer base, you would think Twitter would want to ensure their users' perspectives were represented somewhere in their leadership, right?

"With my departure, Twitter no longer has any managers, directors, or VPs of color in engineering or product management," Leslie said in the same interview quoting that SVP.

Here's an even more stupefying fact: while over a quarter of all U.S. women internet users have a Twitter account, at the time of Mileys' interview there were exactly zero women on its board of directors.[3]

None.

In response to the outcry, the board brought on Debra Lee, chairman and CEO of BET, in 2016. (Black and female: what media analysts call a twofer.) More recently, they added another woman to the board, British entrepreneur Martha Fox.

Did Debra and Martha land their positions because they were women? Of course they did—that was the whole point. Are there thousands of other women out there who landed their position or were tasked with their responsibilities because of their sex? Again, yes.

Especially when someone else has screwed up.

## Falling off the Glass Cliff

As if becoming a female executive isn't hard enough, when some of us make it, we face an entirely new challenge: We get to become the poster child of a corporation's gender-equity commitment.

Or its scapegoat, depending on how things go.

You might have read about Michelle Ryan and Alex Haslam's eye-opening 2005 study "The Glass Cliff."[4] They surveyed the top 100 companies on the U.K.'s Financial Times Stock Exchange and found that if a company had experienced volatility or performed poorly in the previous five months, it was more likely to appoint a woman as CEO than a man. Their research findings were supported in 2013 when Alison Cook and Christy Glass analyzed all Fortune 500 CEO transitions over a 15-year period and found that women and other minorities were more likely to be named CEO when the companies were underperforming.[5]

Michelle and Alex's research has its share of detractors. Unsurprisingly (for me, at least), women are more likely to recognize and accept the validity of the phenomenon, while men are more likely to downplay its prevalence or deny its existence altogether.[6]

But let's look elsewhere to see if we can find similar examples.

Alison and Christy wanted to see if the glass cliff applied to ethnic minorities as well as women; their research suggests it does. Among other examples, their study on NCAA men's basketball looked back over 30 years and found that, if a team was losing, it was more likely to choose a minority head coach. These same coaches also had shorter tenures than their white peers by about a year.

Once we start looking at women being appointed CEO at prominent companies, we can see this pattern emerge for ourselves:

- Anne Mulcahy, the first female CEO at Xerox . . . while the company was on its way to bankruptcy
- Marissa Mayer, the first female CEO at Yahoo! . . . while it was barely surviving against rival Google
- Carly Fiorina, the first female CEO at Hewlett-Packard . . . while it was desperately trying to reinvent itself in the digital age

- Mary Barra, the first female CEO at General Motors . . . who shortly thereafter was forced to issue safety recalls on more than 30 million cars and testify before Congress about the related deaths
- Patricia Russo, the first female CEO at Lucent Technologies . . . which was bleeding money at the time
- Jill Abramson, first female executive editor at *The New York Times* . . . when newspapers were going bankrupt all around the world
- Sallie Krawcheck, CEO of Merrill Lynch's wealth management division after its acquisition by Bank of America . . . which came just weeks after the BoA CEO tried to cancel the deal, fearing Merrill Lynch was in far worse financial shape than previously thought

Why?

If you sit on a board of directors of a multinational and you know the company is in trouble, why are you more likely to appoint a woman to lead it—especially when, statistically, women are overwhelmingly viewed as less competent than men?

Is it because you've suddenly had a change of heart and believe that a woman is the best person for the job? Do you believe that women are more nurturing and therefore a better fit for a troubled company? Do you believe that a woman can do a better job than a man?

Or, if we look at the glass cliff more broadly, why are minorities more likely to be tapped to run for a likely-to-lose office, be peer-selected to argue a stacked law case, or be approached to lead a losing basketball team? Is it because you have more faith in a black man to turn around the team? Because you believe a Latino woman can better argue the case? Because you believe that an Arab Muslim has a better chance of being elected than a white Christian?

I wish I could believe that. I wish I could live in a world where merit earned women and minorities the top leadership spots at companies. But the facts simply don't support it, much less common sense.

A 2013 study by Strategy& (formerly Booz & Co.)[7] found that women CEOs are more likely to be fired than men (38 percent vs. 27

percent, respectively). In Cook and Glass's 15-year survey of Fortune 500 CEO transitions, they found that, once a minority failed to turn around the company, the board was more likely to appoint a white man as CEO, something they called the "savior effect."[8]

(Of course, plenty of glass cliff women have been fired even after successfully turning the company around, like Patricia Russo at Lucent Technologies.)

Some scholars have offered less nefarious explanations for the phenomenon. One with merit: Women often don't have insider information, and so they don't realize how bad the situation is. Their buddies may have warned off all the better-connected candidates. It's insider trading without the stock options.

Another explanation put forth is that, even if the minority candidate knows the situation isn't great, she may believe that "something's better than nothing." Even if it's going to be a challenge, at least it's a chance to spread her wings. When is she likely to get another shot at being CEO?

If you do run the company off the glass cliff, though, you're less likely to get another shot.[9] I mean, who wants the person who ran HP into the ground to sit on their board of directors?

Then again, they may want you just because you're a woman.

**"What's a queen without her king?"**
"Well, historically speaking, more powerful."

—Unknown

## Do We Really Need Quotas? Apparently.

In 2012, German Chancellor Angela Merkel said she was losing patience with the private sector's efforts to increase female representation in its upper ranks. "If they do not respond faster, there will have to be legislation," she said.

Like me, Merkel was frustrated with the glacial change of pace in gender equity. Like me, Merkel saw that one of the only things that would actually galvanize change in the boards of public companies was quotas. Unlike me, Merkel had the power to implement those—and eventually did so.

Taking the threat seriously, German-based Daimler AG named former Avon CEO Andrea Jung to its supervisory board shortly thereafter. Its annual report (released after the chancellor's remarks) set an explicit quota of 20 percent of women to fill its senior executive roles by 2020.

As far back as 2003, Norway enacted legislation requiring public companies to have at least 40 percent of board seats held by women. Consequently, it has the highest percentage of women-held board seats in the world. The governments of Finland, Iceland, Denmark (you have to love our Nordic brethren), France, and Spain have also set quotas. In 2015, Merkel made good on her promise: Germany now has a quota of 30 percent for the number of women on public boards.

The ever-practical Netherlands set board quotas with a time limit; they wanted to make sure the experiment works as desired without any unintentional consequences. I think they can take the expiration date off, though. Plenty of research supports the fact that, yes, having women on the board of directors helps; see the numbers below (studies included for convenience):

- Better gender balance on boards leads to better financial performance in Latin American companies (McKinsey & Co., "Moving Women to the Top: McKinsey Global Survey Results," 2010).[10]
- Mixed-gender boards outperform all-male boards (Credit Suisse, "The CS Gender 3000: Women in Senior Management," 2014; McKinsey & Co., "Diversity Matters," 2015).[11]
- Women-led hedge funds perform in-line or exceed men's (KPMG, "Women in Alternative Investments Report," 2016; Rothstein Kass, "Women in Alternative Investments: A Marathon, Not a Sprint," 2014).[12]
- The Fortune 500 companies with the highest proportion of women in leadership did better than the firms with the lowest (Catalyst Information Center, "Why Diversity Matters," 2013).[13]

The evidence for inclusive boards is mounting.

Perhaps the most telling study, though, comprises 21,980 firms headquartered across 91 countries. It found that a company that went from having no female senior executives to having 30 percent resulted in a 15 percent increase in net revenue. It found a weaker effect with women appointed to the board, and no effect whether the CEO was a man or woman. The greater economic payoff isn't in getting women into the boardroom (though it does pay) but in getting women into the C-suite.

I used to be against mandated quotas. Achievement should be based on merit, not sex. Quotas skip over doing something about the real problem of equal access. But they are the only thing that has really moved the needle on female representation at the very top.

As I cited in Chapter 1, at our current rate we're not looking at wage parity until the end of the century. I don't know about you, but I can't wait that long: I'll be dead.

## Checking the Chick Box

Most of the women in my doctoral research acknowledged that one of the reasons they got in the door was the fact they were female; the company got to "check the chick box," as one of them said.

Sophie Vandebroek freely admits that she only went to work as an engineer because of affirmative action. A recruiting firm looking through a resume database wanted someone who had a high GPA in a computer science-related degree . . . and was a woman. They offered Sophie her first engineering position.

Another woman told me she'd been tapped as a board member because they needed someone "who'd been CEO of a software company based in Silicon Valley and was a woman."

These ladies "only got that job because she's a woman." What about their credentials? Their experience? Most important in the C-suite and especially at the board level, what about their networks? At that level, they have relationships with some pretty incredible people through their work. They were and are qualified. A program or quota

# Neuter the Performance Review

Paola Cecchi-Dimeglio at Harvard, as well as Shelley Correll and Caroline Simard at Stanford, has begun looking into the differences in performance reviews for men vs. women.[14]

Performance reviews are rife with opportunity for unconscious bias because they are so often based on the subjective judgments of the reviewer about the employee. As you would expect (or, at least, you would after seeing the data we've discussed so far), reviews for women team members are often couched in terms based on gender stereotypes: "She needs to assert herself more with clients." Comparable feedback for men was phrased in a more positive light: "Once he becomes more assertive, he'll be an invaluable member of the engineering sales team."

Or, as Correll and Simard's article said, women's feedback was "vague."

To combat this tendency, the researchers suggest:

- Creating objective criteria to evaluate against, not just employing a grading system for the sake of reporting

- Making sure the feedback has a purpose: How does it move the employee, the team, and/or the company closer to their respective goals?

- Giving feedback more frequently: Instead of doing an annual or quarterly review, consider monthly or even weekly reviews (this is also the preferred frequency for millennials)

- Using tech to automate and standardize evaluations

or box-to-be-checked was needed to get them in the door to be vetted, but it was their skills that got them the job.

As I pointed out at the beginning of this chapter, plenty of CEOs landed their positions partially because they're tall, fit, and handsome. Their physical characteristics played an enormous role in their rise to the top. Most venture capital goes to white guys; their ethnicity plays an enormous role in their rise to the top. Most family businesses are passed on to other family members; their DNA plays an enormous role in their rise to the top. The average man makes higher wages than his female equivalent; his gender plays an enormous role in him coming out on top.

> **"Some women who act more like men—there's no femininity to them. They come in a room, start swearing like a sailor, and are forceful—not because that's their personality, but because that's what they've been taught to do."**
>
> —Dissertation study participant

But are their genetics the only reason these men achieved what they did? If you asked them, I promise they'd swear only their own blood, sweat, and tears accounted for their success. The numbers, of course, say otherwise.

Our rule breakers accept the fact that their gender was a factor—but it wasn't the only factor. They didn't get where they are just because they're women, any more than tall, dark, and handsome got where he is just because he's easy on the eyes.

# business maven

S enior tech executive and boardmember Jo-Ann Mendles has played a pivotal role in so many enterprise-level turnarounds that I could spend weeks with her and still feel it wasn't enough time to learn all I want to. But what impresses me more is her purposeful yet pragmatic approach toward business. She embodies mindful disruption at its best. The endgame is never far out of sight. She knows how to bring people together and get them rowing in the same direction.

*You have worked in multiple business sectors. How have you approached the structure of traditional organizations during that time to achieve the success you have today?*

I don't believe there's one "system." The system you find yourself in varies by the nature of the organization, such as a public corporation vs. a private equity firm, whether the strategy is led by the board or management, whether it's entre-preneurial in nature or risk-averse, and more.

In order to successfully maneuver through any given sys-tem, I've had to hone what I call a "portfolio of styles." I am being authentic to myself while at the same time accretively adapting to operating models and cultures. Sharpening acu-men to create value within varied business models requires both deliberate and opportunistic risk taking.

*Would your "portfolio of styles" be analogous to having your own fashion sense but dressing for the occasion?*

I think that analogy works.

*Let's talk about the "deliberate" part of that.*

For me, there are three dimensions to being deliberate.

The first is to be intentional about gaining diverse expe-rience. I spent 20 years in a productive, rewarding corporate career that I'd had since university. Then I made a conscious decision to embark on a different journey. I didn't know what I didn't know, but I knew I wanted something more and some-thing different than what I'd experienced up to that point.

I went from being a predictable, well-compensated senior executive into what I call my entrepreneurial period. That's really where I expanded my experience across all sorts of different structures and sizes of enterprises. It was a constant roller coaster. Much of the time, I was an interim C-level exec-utive. What you learn in an interim role is that from day one you have to deliver results but at the same time work yourself out of the role. This kind of journey isn't for everyone, but it really perfected my dexterity and gave me an immeasurable learning experience.

The second aspect is being deliberate about your pro-fessional brand. I was fortunate to start my career in a large organization where I had the opportunity to have different assignments about every 18 to 24 months. I found that I enjoyed being able to pick up a business in its current state and continue to deliver on its commitments, but at the same time determine the state it needed to become and then bring the operation to that stage. As I went through my entrepreneurial period, I gravitated to the same kind of opportunities: start it, grow it, change it, restructure it, globalize it. It's been important to me to be able to gain credibility from the inside by demonstrating an ability to deliver on the business while changing the business.

The third dimension—and this is related to what I just said—is going after profit-and-loss roles or a business core responsibility. I think this is particularly important as a woman because I was able to not only broaden my business expertise but to demonstrate delivering an objective result. The numbers are the numbers: top-line revenue, profitability, market growth—those aren't subjective measures. It provided me with a track record of objective performance. As such, it positioned me to be in an inner circle in terms of having more ability to effect change. But being a P&L owner incurs a lot of risk. If you don't deliver on the numbers, you're out the door. But typically in a company, whoever holds the money wields a lot of power. It was a deliberate choice on my part to go after P&L roles as opposed to staff roles.

Again, these are things that have worked for me, but they're not necessarily the only pathways to success.

### What do you mean by being "opportunistic"?

I don't mean it in a negative way, as in taking advantage of people. It's about taking advantage of circumstances that present themselves.

In my career, I've had plenty of times where my boss said, "And next, you're going to—." In those situations, accepting the responsibility doesn't mean passively accepting it, despite it not being my choice. Some of those opportunities that were brought to me turned out to be some of the best in my career.

On the other hand, as I said, I have been proactive about some of those opportunities. I don't like generalizing, but women in business don't tend to display the trait of asking, "What do I want? Where do I want to go?"

Women more often ask, "Am I qualified? Do I think I can do the job?"

For some reason, I just don't think that way. I've always felt like I would adjust course as necessary. I knew I would learn from my peers, my colleagues, my clients, the market, etc. I'm comfortable with ambiguity and making decisions based on imperfect information.

By opportunistic, I mean embracing opportunity, whether it's something placed upon you or something you seek out on your own.

### Perhaps just as important: What hasn't worked?

Taking the stance of being right and seeking deserved credit.

I remember the time I was a newly promoted executive, and in a certain situation, I was adamant that I was right about the stance I'd taken. I went full force and staunchly defended my view. Two years later, it turned out that I was right . . . but boy, did I have backlash from taking such a strong position. I learned the hard way that in some situations being right is not necessarily the best course forward. The better approach would have been one in which we could have mobilized key constituents to move forward. Making progress is better than fighting resistance. It's nice to be right, but it's not always effective.

On taking an absolute position on receiving credit: Again, I don't like generalizing, but I've consistently found all over the world that women tend not to take credit for their accomplishments. I'm competitive and I have something of an ego, so early in my career seeing someone else get or take the credit for a result I accomplished annoyed me to no end. I wanted to make sure the record was always set straight.

It is important to pick the situations where it does need to be set straight, but if your real focus is on outcomes—if you want to get results and have people come around to your way of thinking so they can get behind it—then getting the credit isn't as important as becoming known as someone who can successfully get things done.

*Let's return to your portfolio of styles. You spoke about being deliberate and opportunistic; now, let's talk about the flexibility you alluded to.*

There are three things I try to be aware of at all times: physicality, situation, and culture.

I'm a petite female. Early in my career, I was less aware of that. These days, I'm more mindful of how our physical presence affects others' perception. If I walk into a room filled with men, I'll make it a point to make myself seem larger: I'll be the first to extend my hand, I make sure I deliver a firm handshake, I lean in at the table, I'm cognizant of my voice projecting, I take up more room, or whatever else I need to do to ensure my presence is felt. Now, in some countries, this isn't as much of an issue because there I'm not comparatively small. In those instances, I don't need to be so mindful of my presence.

The second way I'm aware of how I communicate is by being appropriate to the situation. That encompasses behavior, my role in the situation, the venue and medium, and even how I present myself. How I dress and act in the corporate boardroom is going to be different than if I'm going into a warehouse.

The third is to be culturally aware. Every culture has different norms, but there is an additional dimension when it comes to being a woman. For example, in running P&L businesses, if a client requested the most senior executive for a meeting, I always considered the client's culture. If it made sense, I'd ask one of the men on my team to take the lead. In those circumstances, challenging cultural norms would not have achieved the outcome I wanted.

You once called me a "pragmatic disrupter." I'd like to think that's exactly what I am.

↗   ↗   ↗

I absolutely love Jo-Ann's portfolio concept. It's a beautiful analogy of how to embrace our authentic self while remaining aware of the practical considerations of a given situation. In Chapter 3, we talked about "covering": the need to minimize certain traits or characteristics to blend in with the group.

The concept of having a portfolio of styles that reflect ourselves while being appropriate for a scenario is similar to that. We wear different outfits for a girls' night out vs. a family event vs. those days when we have to be in a car or an airplane all day. It's the same with running a meeting vs. being invited to a client event.

Jo-Ann's approach seems like a mature, savvy one. Contrast it with those women (or men) who go out of their way to let everyone know everything: their political stance, their religious beliefs, their sexual identity, their relationship status, their childhood, how they believe the company should be run, and more. They have one "outfit" they wear all the time, rain or shine, regardless of circumstances.

I'm sure plenty of feminists would balk at Jo-Ann allowing a junior associate to take the lead in a male-dominated culture. They would want even more to take the lead at that meeting, just to challenge the culture's gender stereotype. But Jo-Ann weighs the costs and benefits, and then deftly maneuvers around other people's prejudices to achieve her goals. When you're a woman who leads disruption, you figure this out pretty quickly: there is no one right way to get to the finish line. The opportunity lies in knowing what to use for your natural leadership style, your strengths, and the context of the environment.

Jo-Ann knows how to play her hand and win the game.

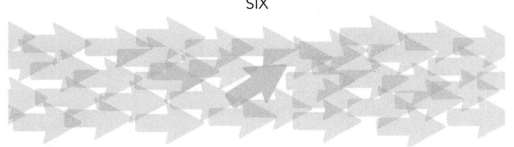

# take the damn job!

*"She was twelve years old when she told Eddie Willers that she would run the railroad when they grew up. She was fifteen when it occurred to her for the first time that women did not run railroads and that people might object. To hell with that, she thought—and never worried about it again."*

—AYN RAND, *ATLAS SHRUGGED*

After becoming CEO of IBM, Ginni Rometty related how earlier in her career a senior executive had outright offered her the job he was about to vacate. She turned him down, saying, "It's too early. I'm not ready. Just give me a few more years."

When she went home and told her husband what had happened, he asked, "Do you think a man would have answered the question that way?"

She realized he was right. The next day, she took the job.

There's a saying I heard when I was researching my dissertation: "When a woman doesn't know something, she takes a class; when a man doesn't know, he takes the job."

Usually, a man's attitude is, *If I don't know it, I can always figure it out later.* Women, on the other hand, are generally like Ginni: *Oh, I don't know it, so I'd better learn it before I take the job.*

We focus on perfection when we should just focus on progress.

> **"**My grandfather once told me that there are two kinds of people: those who do the work and those who take the credit. He told me to try to be in the first group; there was much less competition there.**"**
>
> —Indira Gandhi

## Forget Confidence—Focus on Competence

In my dissertation research, a woman told me, "I'm a golfer, but there is really a big difference between women and men on things like golf. Men will go play business golf even if they're awful at golf. Women only play business golf if they're pretty good because they don't want to be embarrassed. And it's dramatic, the difference. I've played in golf outings where there are a lot of men that are awful. And there are never any women that are awful because they will decline the invitation."

This little observation encapsulates women's chicken-and-egg problem: Confidence comes from competence, but we can't acquire true competence without applying ourselves, and we can't truly apply ourselves without accepting the challenge . . . which we don't want to do until we're confident in our abilities.

Many women take the long road: they gradually acquire an overwhelming amount of competence until they feel confident enough to accept another set of responsibilities.

I believe this is one of the areas where we as a gender truly do ourselves an injustice. The faster way to get where you want to go is to ignore the voice in your head screaming about your lack of confidence. Develop your capabilities and dive headfirst into the challenge. You can worry about finding confidence later. You need to become comfortable with uncertainty.

## Embrace the Unknown

Wendy Foster was a senior executive at AOL before she stepped into the role of CEO at Big Brothers Big Sisters of Massachusetts Bay. The responsibilities were enormous. Not only did she switch from the high-tech private sector to the nonprofit space, but she was suddenly reporting to a board of directors and acting as the public face of a well-known charity.

She said she felt the pressure not just for competence but mastery. She was conditioned to believe that she was supposed to know all the answers from day one on the job. Her board knew her background and knew she had the competence to figure out the challenges a growth CEO faces. It was up to Wendy to grow into the chief exec she wanted to be, not the leader she perceived that her board was looking for to lead the nonprofit to new heights.

Wendy's experience is common. The higher up a person climbs, the less clear cut the rules and expectations are . . . and yet the more you're expected to know exactly what to do. The difference between men and women, as gender studies have shown, is that "men take the job; women take the class." That is, men are more likely to aim for and accept a job for which they feel unprepared. They figure they can attain competence as they go. Women, on the other hand, are more likely to first acquire skills and training. Once they attain competence, they'll aim for the promotion or new position.

The systemic bias in corporate culture encourages this—sometimes explicitly. Several highly qualified females executives I know have been directed to take Stanford's class on becoming an effective board member before putting themselves in the running for board positions—a class not required of their male counterparts. Yet these women were fully credentialed and connected at all the right levels, making each of them fantastic board candidates—even more qualified than many of their male peers. There's nothing wrong with the class. In fact, I happen to like the curriculum. It's been such a good resource that it's now available at many other top tier schools. But the certification would serve the whole board, not just incoming women. As it is, it's another example of blatant sexism.

My research and experience shows that disrupters who reach their goals firmly believe in their own competence. That's one of the primary drivers of their success. However, they virtually all experience "impostor syndrome." They worry that they don't have what it takes to meet new challenges.

One of the reasons I've presented in-depth conversations with the all-stars throughout this book is to help you realize that if you feel imposter syndrome, you're not alone. Not by a long shot. A lack of confidence is normal.

Confidence comes from having faced something before. When you're a leader or a change-maker, though, you don't have the luxury of experience. Instead, you have to rely on your capability: You may not know what you're doing, but you can be confident in your ability to figure it out.

The top two things my doctoral research participants said were key to overcoming barriers (such as gender bias and self-imposed obstacles) were competence and mindset.

But how do you acquire them? Let's talk about some of the most common mindsets that limit women in business, as well as how to get not just more experience but the right kind of experience—the kinds of roles and responsibilities that will eventually take you where you want to go.

## Impostor Syndrome: The 800-Pound Gorilla in Your Brain

Impostor syndrome is, by far, the most common trait the women I've talked to and coached have experienced. *Every* woman who's attained a modicum of success worries that one day, someone will realize she doesn't know what she's doing. The common refrain I hear: "I'm afraid they'll find out I'm a fraud!" Newsflash: *everybody* is winging it.

I work harder and longer hours than most people I know. I have a lot of challenges to overcome. I'm never the most educated/worldly/articulate/attractive/intelligent person in the room, but I am the hardest-working person in the room. It's my modus operandi.

Humans are perfectly imperfect. Now that we get that, let's move on. No one is great at everything, and everyone is great at something. The focus on confidence, where the "not good enough" belief perpetuates and where experience is the only perceived indicator of capability, needs to be replaced by a focus on competence. Competence drives out impostor syndrome by addressing it head-on. Women who understand that they have the capability to figure things out, even when they aren't "the best," know that they've earned a place in the room and at the table.

## Be Aware When You're the Only Woman in the Room

It took a class on feminist leadership theory for me to finally realize, *What have I been thinking? How have I been so blind to the obvious?! How did I not see that I'm almost always the only woman in the room!?* It makes a difference. I have to be better prepared and do more to demonstrate my competence and capability than my male counterparts. I shouldn't; it's outright sexism. But it's the reality nevertheless.

It reminds me of the time a chief diversity officer admitted she still battles unconscious bias. While she was flying over Greenland, the Airbus A380—the largest passenger aircraft in the world—encountered some turbulence. (If you've ever had to fly over Greenland, you know exactly what I'm talking about. It's *always* turbulent.) The captain made some reassuring announcement; a woman, as it turned out.

The diversity officer's immediate reaction was, *I really wish it was a man. I hope she can do this.*

Afterward, she realized how ridiculous her fear was—as if the captain needed to get out and physically carry the plane through the air. There's no logical reason a man would automatically be more qualified to handle turbulence than a woman. And that was her point: Even someone as attuned to those irrational feelings as she is still experiences unconscious bias. But instead of punishing or shaming herself for her automatic assumption, she acknowledged it. Once you become aware, your unconscious bias turns conscious. Your bias, if found to be unsupported, eventually eradicates itself from your brain— but only if your decision-making and reasoning are interrupted for a moment of true clarity.

## Don't Assume Others Know More Than You

What share of Fortune 500 CEOs went to Ivy League schools? While you're thinking about your answer, remember that we're talking about AT&T, GE, JPMorgan Chase, Boeing, Intel, Pfizer, Dow, and other such companies, with gross profits larger than the GDP of many countries. We're talking about the elite executives at the helm of these business giants.

The first time someone posed this question, I thought I'd guess provocatively low: "Half?" Nope. Barely a third. Which means almost two-thirds went to more modest schools, like Texas A&M, the University of Tennessee, and the University of Arkansas.[1] Don't assume that other people necessarily have more ability or education than you.

And don't let the path you took define you. You choose how to define it. Take my route to higher learning. Despite having the chops to be accepted to some of the best colleges and universities on the planet, I couldn't take advantage of the opportunity. My parents' salaries were somewhere between "sorry, you don't make enough to afford this place" and "sorry, you make too much to qualify for financial aid." I had to enroll at a smaller but more affordable college.

For my MBA, I was married and working, so Chris and I could afford for me to go to Richmond University's prestigious School of Business in London. But when it came time to pursue my doctorate, I couldn't quit my job. Chris was at home with the girls by then and mine was the sole source of income. On top of that, I had to travel extensively. That necessitated a flexible, online degree program. The only one that fit my circumstances was the University of Phoenix. One saving grace that helped ease my own concerns about the quality of the program vs. a traditional classroom approach were the opinions being voiced by such leaders as Clay Christensen. After studying the early adopters of online education like the University of Phoenix, he stated that not only was online learning a viable method of education but that if brick-and-mortar institutions didn't follow suit, they'd be facing serious competition. His predictions, of course, were spot on.

So I used to worry about people scoffing at my online degree when they could whip out a degree from some Ivy League. That was never in the cards for me. Today, however, my professional work and doctoral research speak for themselves. I don't need to stand on the credibility of the world's most prestigious institutions, despite now having earned certifications from Harvard and MIT.

My work and achievements overshadow whatever academic pedigree I lack. I don't allow my previous temerity about the source of my higher education define what I'm capable of. My path may not have been traditional, but I've never let it determine the path ahead.

> **"***I've worked with a lot of people who had six degrees from Ivy League schools, but they can't parallel park.***"**
>
> —Dissertation research participant

## Act "As If"

Don't fake it 'til you make it. Not only does that reinforce your belief that you are an impostor, but it undermines your confidence and sense of authenticity as well. Don't pretend to be something you're not.

But you can act "as if." Act as if you believe you are up to the task. Act as if you feel comfortable taking on the challenge. Act as if you're worthy of the promotion. Act as if you're capable of landing the contract. You wouldn't be in the position if you didn't have the necessary abilities. Remember that you most likely had to beat out a boatload of men for your job. You earned it. And if you didn't, you soon will.

## Budget Your Energy More Than Your Time

Where do you invest your energy? Like a financial budget or time budget, we have a finite amount of enthusiasm or mental capacity. Where are you investing yours?

When you finish a task, ask yourself, "Did that take too much time?" Maybe not . . . but did it take too much energy? Do you feel energized after doing something? Or do you feel drained? Just as you can learn to manage your time, you can decide where to invest your energy.

## Practice, Practice, Practice

Play out scenarios. What would happen if absolutely everything went wrong? What would you do if everything went your way? What could you do with half the support or resources you need? How would you recover from a total failure?

By running through these various scenarios, you're mentally attacking the fears and self-imposed barriers we've been talking about throughout this book. The more preparation you do, the more control you'll feel, regardless of how things actually turn out.

I've learned that, to be magnificent on stage, I need to run through a number of practice sessions. I hate practicing, but boy do I feel competent when I know exactly what I'm talking about.

> **"Be so good they can't ignore you."**
>
> —Steve Martin

## Go Where You're Welcome

Try to find a team, a division, or even another company where you don't have to be a trailblazer. Go where other women are, especially at the helm. CCTV-America (now CGTN America) business reporter and anchor Shraysi Tandon once pointed out in an interview how many women her company employed in prominent positions, from directors and managing editors to anchors and producers. A company

### DiversityInc's 21 Best Companies for Women

DiversityInc's Top 50[2] is already a who's who of corporate diversity (applicant companies must employ at least a thousand people). But after analyzing their 2015 survey data further, they found 21 companies that were outstanding places to work as a woman. In alphabetical order, they are:

1. Abbott
2. AbbVie
3. Accenture
4. Deloitte
5. Eli Lilly
6. EY

7. Kaiser Permanente

8. Kellogg

9. KeyCorp

10. KPMG

11. Marriott International

12. MassMutual Financial Group

13. MasterCard

14. Novartis Pharmaceuticals

15. PricewaterhouseCoopers

16. Prudential Financial

17. Sodexo

18. Target

19. Time Warner

20. Wells Fargo

21. Wyndham Worldwide

For their 2017 survey, DiversityInc focused more on upper-level representation, promotion, etc., and rated these nine companies as best for executive women (in ranking order):

1. EY

2. Northrop Grumman

3. Cummins

4. KPMG

5. Marriott International

6. J.C. Penney

7. Kellogg

8. PricewaterhouseCoopers

9. United Continental

If you're looking for an organization that values your contributions, you'd do well to start with one that makes gender equity a key component of its business success.

like this welcomes diverse perspectives; working there will be a much easier path than going where you're the only woman in the room.

## Say Yes to the Right Things

Yogi Berra said, "When you come to a fork in the road, take it." If you've defined your own finish line, when you're confronted with a decision, the criterion is simply this: Will it move you toward your goal or away from it?

If you know what you're working toward, you can work backward from there. Do you really have to accept that task or assignment? What would happen if you realized that a project wasn't going to move you closer to that finish line . . . and said no?

We women are always being told to say yes to every big opportunity. The key is not to take on every big-risk, big-reward project. It's to say yes to the right initiatives that will accelerate you achieving your goals while challenging your skills, maximizing your strengths, and cultivating powerful relationships.

A few rules of thumb come directly from the entrepreneur's handbook (because make no mistake, to achieve success as you have defined it, you will need to entrepreneur the heck out of your life). If it makes you afraid, if it moves you out of your comfort zone and into unknown waters, then it probably is the right direction for you. At the very least, it's a growth opportunity, and the more experience and competencies you have under your belt, the more options you have and the more opportunities you can take advantage of.

Here's the flip side of the coin: Is the decision you face driven by your fear of disappointment or loss, your worry of being perceived as unacceptable, or your need for validation? Are you moving in this direction simply because it's what your friends, family, co-workers, peers, or others expect of you? Are you too ashamed to turn back now? Will changing directions be an implicit admission of failure—something your self-image just can't handle?

## Reinvent Yourself. Again.

Don't just take the fork in the road; take the *hard* one.

When I went to college, I chose one far away from home where I knew absolutely no one. Even more important, no one knew me.

I grew up spending a lot of time with my father's side of the family, a large Irish-Catholic family where cousins, aunts, and uncles numbered well into the double digits. Regardless of my personality, ambitions, or flaws, I already had a lifetime of expectations that came simply from being born. I wanted to start fresh, in an environment with few assumptions about who or what I was supposed to be.

It sucked.

I did, however, eventually make some great friends (some lifelong). It taught me how to survive and adapt in a situation where I had exactly nothing going for me. Most important, it taught me the value of going where no one knows your name so that you are free to reinvent yourself instead of having to be the person others see you as.

I've kept this habit as I've gotten older. I am forever landing in situations where I am in way over my head, where I know almost no one or nothing, and where I have to figure it out as I go along (the old joke of building the airplane while flying it) while striving to create a better version of myself.

I started my professional career at SAP in my 20s and stayed there for years, but eventually decided to leave for IBM, where I could start fresh with a new challenge. I left IBM to lead a large-scale marketing transformation at an information services firm, an industry I knew nothing about, before taking on my own business and returning to work with SAP. I came back into the SAP ecosystem in a completely different capacity. Like so many professionals before me, I found it easier to leave and come back than to stay on the same track.

Although I didn't realize it at the time, I was following in the footsteps of the successful women we're profiling here. Perhaps the most important thing you can do to rapidly succeed in business as a woman is to continually take the jobs, roles, responsibilities, and projects that scare the hell out of you.

> **"The professional loves her work. She is invested in it wholeheartedly. But she does not forget that the work is not her."**
>
> —Steven Pressfield

As I said in my dissertation, "increased self-confidence came from continual personal development." Our overachievers continually pushed themselves out of their comfort zones and into areas where they had little demonstrable competence—only a demonstrable capability to perform.

To list just some of their areas of expertise:

- Investment banker
- CIO with go-to-market experience
- Transaction experience as an attorney
- Crafting legislation
- Owned a P&L sheet (which I've done myself; for all those armchair quarterbacks, it's different when it's your ass on the line)
- Successful MNC sales experience
- Enterprise-level internet sales channel
- Ran multiple national TV shows
- Product management with operations background
- Clinical medical trials across multiple countries

When you see their resumes, it's no surprise they were invited to join a board of directors. They're amazingly accomplished. But they didn't stumble into their expertise. They chose the harder jobs, the more disruptive tasks, and the more "stretch" responsibilities.

> "No one is going to get asked to do something because they're a woman. They're going to get asked because they're a competent woman who's done something."
>
> —Dissertation research participant

Our takeaway isn't that we should simply work harder—that we should be the first one to the office and the last one to leave. These women found their own finish lines and created a life around their work (instead of the other way around). When I say they took the more difficult route, I mean mentally and emotionally. They didn't chase titles or favors or paychecks. They sought challenges.

At the same time, they didn't take whatever opportunity happened to present itself. Their pursuits were strategic and intentional. Because they had a clear vision of their finish line, they had a good sense of what sort of challenges would be a stepping stone toward that end and which wouldn't help or would even move them away from it.

Nor did they start from scratch. They didn't, say, try to land a job in manufacturing operations from their current position in tech sales. They found positions where they could quickly leverage their existing skills and/or that complemented their career experience. The phrase, if you will, is "strategic competence."

In Chapter 5, we talked about how none of these women relied on their gender to bypass the qualifications or needs of the board. As one of them said during my dissertation research, "[The board] wanted to be able to check the chick box, but I've never been treated like a diversity candidate. I've always been ultimately picked for my skill set and what I bring to the table. The fact that I happen to be a woman is a bonus."

## Why Companies Need You: The Diversity Advantage

A good friend of mine who works in the medical field found herself at a cocktail party chatting with a hospital executive. Being the gender advocate she is, she turned the conversation to increasing the number of women in medical programs.

To her astonishment, he said, "I don't want women in the surgical department. Look what happened in pediatrics. Look what happened in general practitioner medicine. The minute women come in, everyone's pay goes down."

As sexist as that sounds . . . he's right.

Sociologist Paula England reviewed industry wages stretching back a half century, from 1950 to 2000. She found that when women entered traditionally male jobs (like medicine or wildlife management) in large numbers, wages decreased across the board, even when skills and experience remained the same.

(Of course, when men entered traditionally female jobs, such as computer coding or nursing, wages rose. All things equal, male nurses make $5,100 more than their female co-workers, according to the American Medical Association.[3])

The executive my friend spoke with blamed the effect on women, effectively saying, "Let's keep them out so we can keep our wages up."

Shouldn't the real question be, "Why can't we all make this much money? Why is it that having more women in a profession brings down the pay?" Isn't that what we should be fixing?

Instead, the focus turns to lowering the bar. To allow minorities into their clubs, they have to lower their standards . . . because God knows, we couldn't make it on our own merit. We can't compete with white guys. They're just naturally superior to the rest of us in every way.

Yes, that sounds crazy when you see it in black and white, but listen closely: that's the real argument behind statements like, "We want diversity, but we won't lower the bar," or, "We'd hire more women, if only we could find qualified candidates."

This reminds me of my friend Dr. Caroline Simard, currently at Stanford University's Clayman Institute and former head of research at the Anita Borg Institute (ABI) for Women and Technology. ABI consistently named IBM one of the Top Companies for Women Technologists. In an article for *The New York Times*, she said that at IBM,

> They see their ability to compete in today's marketplace, to approach new markets, and to make money as being tied to diversity. It really is a business imperative and not just a responsibility of HR.

In a 2017 interview with NPR's *Marketplace*, Sallie Krawcheck pointed out that Wall Street didn't see the financial industry's implosion coming because of the "false comfort of agreement . . . It's groupthink. And the way you break groupthink is through diversity."

The numbers back her up. The 2015 study "Professors in the Boardroom" examined S&P firms and found that companies with more academics led to higher acquisition performance, lower discretionary accruals, more patents, and better return on assets.[4] Another 2013 study found that LGBT-friendly companies had higher productivity and profitability—and companies that discontinued such policies saw a corresponding drop in the same metrics.[5] A 2012 Swiss study

## HR as a Gateway to Innovation

While I've made the point that gender equity should be embraced at all levels of organization, I've also made the point that we're dealing with an embedded, systemic, unconscious bias. We're trying to overcome millennia of social and cognitive norms and expectations. That kind of paradigmatic shift takes decades or even generations to move.

But using technology, HR can subvert or even shortcut a lot of those unseen biases. Intel and SAP, among others, have used analytics to uncover pay disparity within their own ranks and then taken corrective action to address those disparities. What a wonderful step in the right direction.

While the U.S., as well as several individual states, has pay equity laws on the books, any HR professional knows these regulations are often so open-ended and vague as to be difficult to implement, much less enforce. Nevertheless, plenty of companies are self-policing to ensure that equal responsibilities and equal results correspond with equal pay, regardless of gender or other personal factors.

You just read earlier that one job ripe for such pay equity analyses is registered nurses, where men earn an average of $5,100 more than women. Researchers found a salary gap existed at all levels of RNs and for all positions (except orthopedics), from the beginning of the data period in 1988 through 2013. Every single year, a male RN made five grand more than a female one—but it took analyzing the data to see that.

HR departments have made impressive progress in finding and recruiting talent based on the match between personal values and corporate culture. That will become increasingly important for companies as we move forward. But it smacks of hypocrisy when a woman constantly hears how important company culture is while she watches her less-qualified, less-experienced male co-worker get promoted ahead of her, or sees her male peer get a higher raise despite her demonstrably better performance.

Put yourself in her shoes: Would those situations affect your motivation? Your loyalty? Your commitment? Would it signal to you that your contributions to the company were less important than your lack of a Y chromosome?

*Working Mother* magazine released a particularly insightful 2015 report entitled "Multicultural Women at Work."[6] One of the questions was "Do you plan to leave your company in the next three years?"

- Twenty-two percent responded "Definitely yes."

- An additional 33 percent responded "Maybe."

- Twenty-nine percent responded "Definitely not."

- Only 16 percent weren't sure.

Please keep in mind these weren't women in traditionally high-turnover positions. All of the nearly 1,800 women were college-educated. Their average household income was six figures, and their average age was 40. More than a third were in management.

By the way, of the 1,746 respondents, 400 identified as white, non-Hispanic. Whatever company you work at, odds are that the women in your company are already thinking about their exit, regardless of their ethnicity and heritage.

What's the number-one reason they want to leave? It's not flexibility in their work schedule. When, where, and how they got their work done were the least important factors in retention.

Nearly two-thirds wanted to leave for better pay. More than half wanted a better opportunity to advance. Only about a third were looking for a better work-life balance.

Unless your organization does something, your management team is going to start looking more homogenous while your best and brightest are walking out the door . . . just because they believe they will be treated better elsewhere—and the research bears them out. As you've seen throughout this book, odds are low that they're getting equitable pay.

Promoting inclusion, addressing micro-inequities, and combating gender stereotypes are all important things that must be addressed. Doing a gender parity analysis to ensure fair compensation? That's a simple step you can take, and yet it's a huge factor in retaining female employees.

Companies are fretting over how to handle millennials, but do you realize we're looking at a work force that for the first time in history comprises five distinct generations? In her *Harvard Business Review* article "Are You Ready to Manage Five Generations of Workers?"[7] cowritten with Jeanne C. Meister, Karie Willyerd broke them down:

- Traditionalists (born before 1946)

- Baby Boomers (born between 1946–1964)

- Gen X (born between 1965–1976)

- Millennials (born between 1977–1997)

- Gen Z (born after 1997)

Consider this: The kids in high school now weren't even born when the Twin Towers fell. That horror is fresh for you and me, but it's history to them, akin to us reading about Pearl Harbor or the *Titanic*.

These generations have five totally different life experiences, cultural references, motivations, and worldviews. While the Traditionalists share pictures of their grandchildren, the Baby Boomers are taking care of their parents and boomerang kids. Meanwhile, the Gen Xers who are juggling jobs and their kids' soccer games roll their eyes at the Millennials taking extended leave to go hiking in Patagonia.

Beyond gender and age, there's ethnicity. Multinational corporations have an amazingly diverse group of skill sets and perspectives to draw from. Rising stars in a company are just as likely to hail from Dublin as from Denver; Singapore as Saigon. And what about sexual orientation? LGBT+ individuals coming into the mainstream adds multiple new dimensions of culture, experience, and perspective.

The more homogenous the decision-makers, the more homogenous the leadership . . . and we've moved beyond homogenous markets. Corporate executives can continue to follow the one-size-fits-all approach to leadership, but their talent pool will continue to shrink, and what's left will stagnate.

> Unless you're using tech to measure, track, and capitalize on these opportunities, you're flying blind. Throwing money at the problem in the form of diversity programs or workplace trainings doesn't help if you're trying to fix the wrong problem.

from *Strategic Management Journal* spanning 32 industries examined diversity by nationality among top management and found that it led to higher firm performance.[8]

The bottom line: diversity *of all kinds* makes companies better.

Think about what a manufacturing executive said in a 2013 *Harvard Business Review* interview about leadership postings: "We know that the men will nominate themselves even if they don't meet all the requirements; the women would hold back."

Don't hold back. Take the damn job. We need you.

# the power of the outsider

Like most of the disrupters in my tribe, Tanya Odom doesn't present her impressive credentials unless they're relevant to the conversation or task at hand. It's not that she downplays them, but she doesn't display them unless they serve a purpose. But to give you context for her story, let me list some of her professional accomplishments and leave it to her to relate her personal journey.

School at Vassar and Harvard. Work with the United Nations and the European Union. Named by Diversity Best Practices as "One of the Five Diversity Thought Leaders to Follow on Twitter." Clients like Google, American Express, and the New York Stock Exchange. Lecturer or adjunct professor at Princeton's Summer Institute, Georgetown, and the University of Cape Town, among others. Delegate to the World Conference Against Racism. Consultant and writer on diversity, equity, innovation, and creativity in the workplace and society.

Basically, she is an all-around all-star who lives and breathes her work. She is a bright light of hope for many in this fight, working on behalf of all of us. No one is left behind. Her passion and her focus sit squarely in the impact she is helping to make and to lead.

### *Tanya, can you share a bit about your amazing background?*

My dad said if he saw my bio, he probably wouldn't come to one of my sessions. On paper, I reek of privilege. It looks like I couldn't possibly relate to the everyday reality of many people.

So most people don't know what to do when I tell them that my parents were the directors of a residential therapeutic drug community center. We lived inside the facility itself. Not a hippie commune, but an urban clinic. My earliest memories are of being cared for and cuddled by this extended family. In fact, my younger sister teases that there are very few pictures of me and her walking; we were always being carried. Later, I learned they were drug addicts and some had criminal records. Sometimes, they had to "go away." As a kid, I was writing letters to people in jail who were family, like aunts and uncles.

Add that on top of the fact that, despite the fact that I look and am always assumed to be white, my father is black and my mother is white, and people really don't know what to do. I don't fit into any neat little box.

I'm always careful to point out that my parents were not in the clinic per se; they worked in the clinic. They were the two directors of Monument Manor and lived on-site. Unfortunately, the center closed when I was seven, so my younger sisters don't have the memories I do, but going into helping professions is still a big part of our family. One of them is a lawyer working in legal aid and the other is a youth development social worker.

### *And it's important to you to share that with people?*

Not really. It's important to me that I don't hide it.

I meet so many people in my coaching practice and in my work where they're hiding a piece of who they are. There's some wonderful research out there that speaks to what we call "covering." It's hiding or not owning a piece of who we are when we're in certain spaces.

Sometimes, I've worked with women of color who have a sense of shame or failure because along their road of life, they've collected some bumps and bruises. The things they experienced do not fit into what other people's world looks like or how those people think the world should look like.

***How do we embrace those parts of who we are? How do we honor those pieces of our identities?***

I love Brené Brown's TED Talk on shame and vulnerability. In order to get to the place where you feel like you belong—she speaks to the concept of "worthiness"—you have to embrace that vulnerability.

I think we have to tell our own stories in ways that support and motivate each other. The idea of diversity lands differently for women of color, women who are lesbians, or those from different socioeconomic backgrounds. These are things that make us diverse, and yet often we're ashamed of sharing those pieces of ourselves, so we cover them up when we're on the job or in a particular social setting.

We need to embrace what makes us different.

***Fast-forward from your childhood to adulthood. It must have been strange to go from your background to Wall Street.***

I got a job in corporate America because of a white ally. She had been doing diversity work for a long time and recruited me into the firm. At the time, I was working in a dropout prevention program to help teens literally stay in school. I had never worked a day in a corporate job.

She said to me, "You will be OK because, one, people are going to think you're white and, two, your education. Please—

you were just working with gang members on the Lower East Side. I think you'll be fine on Wall Street."

During my first week on the job, we had an off-site for the company where they were talking about their P&L, their losses, anticipated earnings, millions of dollars in revenue. I remember thinking it was like I'd gone to Mars: "Where am I?"

The next week, after work I went to Columbia to listen to a lecture by Angela Davis. There I was, listening to her speak about diversity and human rights while I worked as a management consultant on Madison Avenue, where there was an extreme lack of any kind of diversity, be it racial, ethnic, or cultural.

I remember thinking about the juxtaposition of those two realities—these two worlds. What would my co-workers do if they were sitting beside me? Would they even get what she was talking about?

But I'd been hired to address diversity. I didn't know anything about P&Ls, but I did have passion and a commitment for equity and diversity issues. I was comfortable in front of a room. I had, maybe not a clear direction, but a sense of purpose. So as a management consultant with other groups and then in my own firm, I've continued to work toward that purpose.

I couldn't leave my kids behind, though. I still worked with students in schools. I used my vacation days to work with young people in Europe on anti-racism, for example.

Yes, straddling those two worlds has been a weird experience at times, but it is who I am, and is part of my uniqueness.

### What's it like to work on diversity issues today?

You know, people may say they understand diversity, but until you have lived it, and have seen and heard the stories of people around the world, you really might not understand what diversity and inclusion really is, or how important it is.

I was recently in Nairobi doing some sessions around unconscious bias. In my presentation, I often use myself, my identity, and my unconscious biases as an example.

As we talked about visible diversity, cues, and what we know/do not know about a person, I asked, "What did you think about me when I came in the room?"

In some of my sessions, I show a slide of me with my father and share the fact that I'm biracial. After the session, one man walked up to me, took a deep breath, and said, "You know . . . after revealing that . . . I feel like I can trust you more."

I thought, *Here I am in Kenya, working with this global group of people, and this man still feels a distance from people who don't share his reality of being black.* The fact that my dad was black gave him a different connection to me. That says so much about where we are in the world around these topics.

**I think diversity, inclusion, and equity are not often really understood.**

Recently, I have reconnected with one of my former students who is a young man of color. We are now both very involved in each other's lives. He told me at one point that I was like a parent to him. I take that seriously. My world has changed. My awareness of issues of race, inclusion, and equity have been keenly impacted. I went up to his school for parents' weekend. We got a Zipcar, and after dinner, he dropped me off at my hotel, and then he drove back to his dorm.

Just a few minutes later, he called me and said, "I'm back on campus, but the cops just stopped me. There's two police cars. They took my license. Could you just stay on the phone until I get into my dorm?" That call will stay with me for a very long time.

It turned out OK, they let him go, but I was up for the rest of the night. I wasn't scared—I was scared for him. He's a young black man living in the time of Trayvon Martin, Michael Brown, and Alton Sterling. His reality as a college student is very different than many of his peers simply because he's black.

I shared this story recently and had a woman ask, "How is that a work issue?"

It is a work issue. If I was her co-worker and came to work the next day, this would be on my mind. These are the experiences of some of her co-workers. Things like this happen to people all the time, but they don't feel they can say it at work or they don't feel that other people will truly hear it. If you don't experience that reality, it's hard for you to understand what your co-workers go through, much less empathize with them.

Whenever people don't hear these stories firsthand from friends and peers and co-workers—when they get it third-hand and fourth-hand—it's too abstract. They read about these things happening in the paper, or online, or watch it on the news, but they don't see it affecting the people in their lives.

That's part of why I think we haven't made more progress. We do not always know the realities of different people—at work or at home. We do not always think about the historical legacies that have impacted us differently. People who've had things like this happen then might not feel included or safe and cover up those parts of their life. The people they interact with don't see that these stories, these tragedies, these traumas aren't isolated incidents but are parts of many people's past and present.

**_So we need to be both more aware of other people's realities and more comfortable with sharing our own?_**

Yes, but it's not just the big things. There's also a huge impact in the cumulative result of the seemingly inconsequential little things. It is why I really appreciate Mary Rowe's research on micro-inequities. In the 1970s, she did a study on why women of color were leaving the workplace.

Everyone expected her to discover huge problems, such as blatant discrimination or something like that. Instead, what she found drove them out was an accumulation of micro-inequities. This could be something as subtle as interrupting one group of people more than another group, forgetting to include someone in a meeting, rolling your eyes when someone makes a point, or failing to learn how to pronounce their name correctly.

You might brush off just one instance, but it's the cumulative impact that these things have day after day that creates environments where people do not feel included, "seen," and that eventually drives them elsewhere. The research is there: These little things make a difference.

And as far as being more comfortable sharing our own life: I think we want to be more connected. We want to feel that we're connecting with authentic people. I've met some people in person who follow me on Twitter or have read a couple of my articles, and their remark to me is, "You're really the same person that I thought you were."

That's so refreshing because it means that people do respond positively to my vulnerability. It means I am doing, not a perfect job, but a better job of sharing myself with the world. I know that I don't have it all figured out.

In fact, I was talking to a coach one day about my coaching practice and I said, "You know, there are all these other coaches out there promising that they can help people change their lives and how to have the perfect job and the perfect life . . . and I'm just not that together."

She said, "Isn't that the point?"

That's always stuck with me. Yes, my experience looks different than yours. I have a different story. We have different bumps and bruises. The point isn't to cover these scars but to be vulnerable about what makes us uniquely us.

✒ ✒ ✒

I love the balanced distinction Tanya makes between something being important to share with others vs. being so "important to me that I don't hide it."

I also love the fact that, as her dad's comment alludes to, on paper Tanya looks like the perfect Wall Street employee. But when you dig just a little deeper, you find she has this tapestry of a background that makes her uniquely her.

Sometimes I wonder that, if we could all share even just a modicum more vulnerability and transparency about our backgrounds, our insecurities, and our truths, how many of us would sigh in relief knowing that we're not the only one who sees ourselves a certain way?

That was part of my motivation for showcasing these disrupters' lives in more detail. I want more of us to feel a sense of solidarity and connectedness. Tanya and these other women have not only informed my work but they've inspired my life as well.

I hope their stories do the same for you.

# mentoring works! (except when it doesn't)

*"I don't have a mentor or a coach. I have a personal board of advisors. They just don't know I call them that."*

—DISSERTATION RESEARCH PARTICIPANT

U p until very recently, all tampons on the market were designed and sold by men.

Ummm . . . why do men design tampons?

"Here. We have no personal insight into how your body works, but we've designed something uniquely for you that we're sure will solve your problem. You're welcome."

Does that make any sense? Yet that's how it works for men selling tampons. Without up close and personal experience, their perspective is more than laughable; it's downright insulting.

When engineer Ridhi Tariyal came up with the "smart tampon," she and her business partner tried to pitch it to venture capitalists. Inevitably, that meant sitting across the table from men—many of whom had never actually seen a tampon in real life—trying to explain the market potential for a product that would allow women to monitor their fertility and sexual health from the privacy of their own homes.

One investor quoted in a 2016 *New York Times* article about the smart tampon argued that women were only half the population, "so what was the point?" (*Only* half. Don't you love it?) Another investor reimagined it as a product that did not test for STDs but—are you ready for this?—testosterone. A third guy loved the idea of being able to detect STDs . . . so he could test women before he slept with them.

*This* is why men shouldn't be in charge of tampon design.

Can you imagine the outcry if all the condoms in the world were designed by women? If that were the case and the secret was suddenly exposed, these same venture capitalists would have a new company funded, a "just for men" design patented, and a state-of-the-art factory churning out millions of them—all before next weekend.

There's no way men would be satisfied with women-designed condoms. They would think it was crazy for people who have no experience using such intimate products to design something specifically for the male body.

But men control the boardroom and executive suites at consumer product companies, so they see nothing crazy about people who have the wrong genitalia designing products for the opposite sex.

This absurd double standard—and billions of dollars wasted in bad design and lost revenue—will continue to be the reality of business as long as it is dominated by a single gender.

And executives do exactly the same thing with mentor programs.

## The Awful Truth About Corporate Mentor Programs

They don't work.

There. I said it. Hang me. Run me out of town. Kill the messenger.

I am well aware that millions—even billions—of dollars are being spent on developing corporate mentoring programs for women. *Harvard Business Review*'s cover story for July/August 2016 was "Why Diversity Programs Fail" and addressed many of the costs of failed programs to promote diversity, including gender diversity.[1] You would think that as a proponent of women's equity, I would cheer on these initiatives. And I absolutely would . . . if they actually worked.

They sound great. "Let's pair new hires and young professional women with mid-level and upper-level executives. They'll help the newbies emulate the success they've experienced themselves and be the role models for the next generation of women leaders. OK, HR, get that going."

But I've yet to see any significant study showing that these programs by themselves make a dent in gender equity. Unless there's a true cultural shift supporting the initiatives, mentor programs are just window dressing.

The 2013 report "Women as Mentors: Does She or Doesn't She?"[2] found that, of the companies with a formal mentoring program (only a little more than half), women mentors responded that they had received:

- No training: 22 percent
- Low-quality or very low-quality training: 31 percent
- Moderate quality: 28 percent
- High-quality or very high-quality: 20 percent

To put it another way: only one-fifth of one-half of companies provide quality formal mentoring.

In a 2010 study on co-worker groups from Women in Management, women reported having more mentors than their male counterparts.[3] Yet when controlling for industry, work history, stated ambition, and even whether they wanted children, the women received $4,600 less in wages than their male peers. Even with a mentor, they still didn't get what the guys got.

Overmentored. Undersponsored.

You don't have to dig very deep to find the problems. Women often find that their mentors just want them to do more. How many meetings can they attend? How many more presentations can they deliver? How many more projects can they take on? How much more can they travel? While those mentors probably have good intentions, how much does such advice help?

You know what *would* move the needle? Mentoring programs for the white guys at the top. Women like Ursula Burns and Sophie Vandebroek could work one-on-one with the board and the C-suite, showing them how to bring their companies into the 21st century. Instead of continuing with their white, masculine, homogenous business practices, they could learn how to adapt to today's world.

Now that's a mentor program worth pouring billions into.

## Diversity vs. Inclusion

If I hire a "diversity candidate," but I'm fine with all the heads of major projects looking just like me, then I haven't actually changed anything.

I've achieved diversity; my team includes someone who isn't like the rest of us. But if I don't include you in our discussions, consider your point of view, or value your contributions—if I dismiss your ideas, talents, and experience . . . then while you may be physically present, you don't really have a seat at the table. If you have to act like me to succeed, then I wasn't really looking for new ideas; I just wanted a nice picture for the website.

I may have diversity, but I don't have inclusion.

That's why most mentoring and diversity programs don't work. Like everything else big companies do, they use a classic top-down approach: "The big boys are going to figure out how to fix this, guys. Here, look, we've got a program. We need to teach you, train you, and model what we want to see from you. Run off, do what the facilitator says, then get back to work. Problem solved. Next!"

But foisting a mentoring program onto employees just doesn't work. It's imposing the existing corporate culture in a top-down approach instead of incorporating ideas from new employees in a bottom-up technique. It's diversity, but not inclusion.

## What's the Difference?

Diversity does not mean "minority" or "not white and/or male." Diversity means that you have more than one kind of demographic in the proverbial room. If your team is all-male and you bring one woman onboard, you've "achieved" diversity.

A board of directors giving a seat to a woman is diversity. But if that woman's voice isn't heard, then your board of directors is diverse but not inclusive; you've hired a token piece. As I heard one woman say, "I'm afraid of one becoming the new zero."

Diversity is about numbers. Inclusion is about culture. Inclusion manifests in many ways. It could mean that the person from an underrepresented population is included in the conversation. Her views are given due consideration, and her diverse perspective has an impact on the group's final decision. She feels welcomed.

Diversity is usually the first step; inclusion is the second. It should be the other way around. You can have diversity, but without inclusion, the impact of diversity will never be realized and will not last.

Even if the initiative actually opens the participants' eyes to some real problems, when they get back to the office, this is the response they get: "No, we're not going to change. The culture we have here is fine. You need to adapt. Think about accommodating someone other than the type of managers we've been employing here for 50 years? Are you crazy?"

Right. It's not them. It's us.

Every year, DiversityInc makes a questionnaire available that ranks each participating company's diversity metrics. In its 2015 survey, it analyzed the top 50 companies for gender equity and found they all had:

1. Strong, cross-cultural mentoring programs with a high level of senior executive involvement
2. Active women's employee resource groups, used for recruitment, engagement, leadership training, and talent development
3. Flexible workplaces, usually with individualized programs

Of those 50 companies, DiversityInc said 21 stood out as uniquely oriented toward women, as we listed in Chapter 6. Those 21 companies all had above-average female representation (not just compared to the U.S. average but compared to other companies in the top 50) in management and senior executive positions as well as on their boards of directors.

Here's my point: These companies aren't great for female professionals because they have mentoring programs. These companies are already focused on gender equity . . . so they happen to have great mentoring programs.

In short, a mentoring program alone isn't going to fix your gender gap problem. Pouring more money into it won't help. If your company wants to truly help women, it has to address the inherent bias corporate culture has against women.

Trying to get women to the top without changing the structure (i.e., the culture of the company) is like a game of Jenga. The move may work, but it's on a shaky foundation at best.

## When Mentoring Works

Gloria Larson, president of Bentley University since 2007, worked at the Federal Trade Commission for ten years. Her boss there was Commissioner Patricia Bailey, a trailblazer in the organization. She was more than a boss, though: Patricia was a true mentor and advocate, supporting Gloria as she advanced. She points to the commissioner's influence as a major factor in the success she's had in her career. The FTC didn't pair them together because it thought Gloria needed someone to help her career, though; the mentor-protégé relationship happened naturally.

> **"***Lighthouses don't go running all over an island looking for boats to save; they just stand there shining.***"**
>
> —Anne Lamott

Mentoring programs don't work . . . but mentoring works amazingly well. The mentoring I've observed, received, and given to others didn't happen through formal programs. It was often by chance and happenstance. These are almost always informal relationships with little structure.

Two-thirds of the research participants in my dissertation study had mentored other women, helping them move up the ranks, not as programmatic mentors but as informal ones. Like my earlier referenced research participant's walk-and-talk, advice and counsel was usually given ad hoc, whenever the protégé was going through a difficult

## Coach, Mentor, Sponsor, Champion

I like Brenda Reid's description of mentorship. She shares it here:

> Think of someone trying to climb a mountain. If you're coaching them, you're helping them find the strength and willpower so they can go climb the mountain on their own.
>
> If you're mentoring them, you're telling them how to best climb the mountain: what worked for you when you climbed that mountain or how to avoid the pitfalls along the path.
>
> If you're sponsoring them, you brought them to the mountain in the first place.
>
> If you're championing them, you're telling your mountain-climbing team why this person should come along on the climb with all of you.

situation or faced a tough decision. These tête-à-têtes were where the real mentoring took place—not in scheduled progress meetings.

You don't need to wait to be assigned a mentor. Even if you are part of a mentoring initiative, that doesn't preclude you from finding your own. Our heroines picked mentors with whom they connected, whose leadership and management styles they wanted to model and whose success they wanted to emulate. They found someone they identified with and then sought their help.

Your mentors don't necessarily have to know they're mentoring you. In fact, plenty of people shy away from the word. They don't feel they're experienced enough to be someone's mentor. A friend, a shoulder, someone to whom others turn to for advice, yes . . . but a "mentor"?

Many women don't just look inside their own organization for mentors. (That's not even an option for entrepreneurs or freelancers like Heather Boggini.) They'll tap into their social networks or cold-call someone they've heard about.

Your mentors might be even more distant. Plenty of people have "virtual" mentors—thought leaders or role models they study from a distance via their books, articles, or biographies, such as Maya Angelou, Oprah Winfrey, Ruth Bader Ginsburg, Benazir Bhutto, Indira Gandhi, or Gloria Steinem. Or they may be closer to home: my mother, my grandmother Arshalous, and the other women who sacrificed to make mine and my daughters' lives possible.

These mentors—personal or distant—give us an anchor or reference point. They provide perspective and help us figure out how to navigate this crazy journey of life.

# diversity goes high-tech

Dr. Gabriela "Gabby" Burlacu is an industrial organizational psychologist with SAP SuccessFactors. That means she studies work-force trends and challenges and then finds ways for businesses to face them or even take advantage of them via better processes and tech enablement. Gabby represents all that is wonderful, good, and promising from the Millennial generation. Her insatiable curiosity, together with the ingenuity possessed by the work force's first digital natives, has resulted in groundbreaking work on how organizations can address diversity and inclusion opportunities through technology.

*I love that your title is "human capital management researcher."*

I was born in Romania, but my family moved here when I was two. Growing up and then entering the work force, it became pretty clear to me early on that I certainly looked at things differently than my peers and colleagues. And actually, that's true for all of us: We all look at things differently, depending on where we come from, how we grew up, our values—all these things give us a different perspective than others.

I'd been interested in work-force diversity for a long time, but in graduate school I focused on age diversity in particular. Organizations seem so obsessed with Millennials: "The Millennials are coming! What are we going to do to engage the Millennials?!"

But in doing that, they ignore the fact that there are larger numbers of older people working today than ever before in just about every industry. There are a variety of economic and personal preferences driving those demographics. These people are an economic powerhouse in terms of their skill base, productivity, domain expertise, and institutional knowledge. Companies had better figure out how to engage and leverage them.

We are now in a work force where talent and innovation are more important than ever. The "capital" of the new millennium is human capital, and as a consequence managing your human capital is more important than ever.

### Is technology the answer to moving the needle for diversity and inclusion?

HR processes are now ultimately supporting decisions that we make about talent: who we choose to hire, how much we choose to pay, who we choose to promote, etc. Technology can play a role in presenting unbiased information to decision-makers and having them be able to use it to leverage better outcomes for the organization.

The bigger challenge is not in creating the tech to enable these decisions. The real challenge is getting leaders to embrace the need for it in the first place. Investing in this kind of tech sends a strong signal that an organization wants to be more equitable. Business leaders talk about diversity and I truly believe that, for the most part, they believe diversity is important.

But I've also come across those who have a zero-sum perspective: If we elevate women and promote other types of diversity, it means devaluing the talent of the majority—which, of course, is absolutely not the case.

When you tell these leaders, "Look, the system is wrong. It needs to be changed. We need to elevate new kinds of talent. We need fewer people who look like you and more people who don't," they hear, "You succeeded in a flawed system. Your success comes from working in a system that favored people like you over others."

If that's the message they hear, even on a subconscious level, of course it feels demoralizing. Of course it's more of a challenge to get their support. Of course we encounter more rejection.

It's a sensitive topic and one that has many sides and per-spectives. Someone always feels left out, hurt, or condemned. Nothing will change if the conversation doesn't change. How do you change the narrative for these business leaders?

"Why aren't there more women in the boardroom with you?" isn't the best approach.

The better question—and, really, the better focus—is "How can we ensure that we're getting the absolute best peo-ple at the top working for your company?"

If we believe that talent is no respecter of age, gender, or race, and if we believe that diversity drives better business outcomes—and the research demonstrates that it does—then if we use tech to make better human capital management deci-sions, then diversity should naturally follow.

When a chief human resources officer (CHRO) or a chief diversity officer (CDO) attempts to address these issues with technology, they are asking the leaders they support questions such as, "How do you engage your talent via performance management? How do you ensure you're onboarding people correctly?"

Those are important questions, not just for their own sake, but because it challenges most people's ideas on promoting diversity in the workplace. Traditionally, those questions are, "Should we provide training? Should we launch a women's leadership program? Should we recruit and hire based on targets? Should our quota be 40 percent or 50 percent?"

Diversity for diversity's sake is the right philanthropic thing to do, but what drives business decisions are business factors. What has compelled companies to embrace diversity is tying its benefits to the financials. The message is, "Look, you don't have the talent you need. The global work force is becoming more diverse. If you continue hiring and promoting the same way you have, you will run out of the talent you need to compete . . . and here's the financial impact of that mistake."

This was really the same story for HR in the past. Business leaders would ask why they needed to invest in a whole team of people to worry about how to manage all the rest of their people. Once HR professionals were able to financially justify their existence, then having an HR department became the norm.

It is a shame, though, that HR professionals had to financially demonstrate the answer to a question that was essentially "Why should we invest in our people?"

### Talk about the tech around bias.

This may be looking at the world through rose-colored glasses, but I believe that most bias is unconscious bias. In fact, there's plenty of research showing that the perpetrators of bias against women are often other women. This is a systemic issue.

Technology allows us to bring some of these decisions to the forefront to help us detect those times when a decision may have been affected by our own cultural or embedded biases.

One thing technology has been doing for some time is helping to determine salary by looking at a person's position and responsibilities and then comparing it to their peers', not just inside the company but across the industry. That way, we can make salary decisions without the additional lens of gender, age, or race.

HR tech is also viewed as an end-to-end process. Historically, the people who did the hiring never even spoke to the people who did the training and development. Now we know that having a comprehensive HR strategy is a lot more powerful. Technology allows this to happen as a system instead of individual activities done in silos.

So it is with diversity: we need to consider not just how we recruit and hire differently but how we train, develop, and retain differently so that we have the best talent rising to the top.

⌁  ⌁  ⌁

Gabby could not be more right. When it comes to diversity and inclusion, technology does not determine success or failure. Cultural transformation is the answer. Technology simply enables cultural change. It is critical to scaling the change journey and ensuring that the change sticks.

In Chapter 2, I quoted Pat Milligan's talk about how women can start advocating for their own career equity by holding leaders accountable for equitable practices. Imagine if a hiring manager's answer was to show how she uses technology to nudge away unconscious bias when it comes to whom she hires and whom she promotes?

Now *that* would be a game changer.

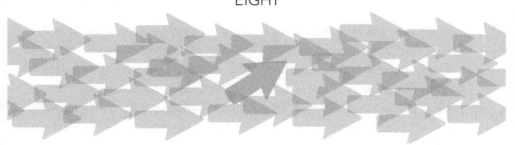

# thrive in the tribe

*"Siamo angeli con un'ala soltanto e possiamo volare solo
restando abbracciati."*
*("We are each of us angels with only one wing, and we can only
fly by embracing one another.")*

—Luciano De Crescenzo

In 1999, the Diana Project—a survey of U.S. venture capital funding—revealed that, of the companies funded by VCs that year, less than 5 percent had even one woman on their executive teams. That is, 95 percent of all VC-funded companies had all-male management.[1]

If 1999 seems like it was just weeks ago (as it does to me), it's easy to recall those heady days. The dotcom bubble had yet to burst, we were two years away from 9/11, the economy was booming, and people couldn't buy tech stocks fast enough.

Silicon Valley was a bunch of computer geniuses who joined new companies and then left to start their own, all in the same week. It was raining money, and venture capitalists couldn't push it into founders' hands fast enough. Since women were virtually nonexistent out there, that 5 percent statistic shouldn't come as a surprise. Everybody knows that VC-worthy companies were run by white guys in their garages, right?

The Diana Project dug a little deeper, though. They concluded there were plenty of fund-worthy, high-growth-potential, women-majority-owned startups with the requisite skills and experience. So why were they systematically overlooked?

> **"**It was we, the people; not we, the white male citizens; nor yet we, the male citizens; but we, the whole people, who formed the Union. And we formed it, not to give the blessings of liberty, but to secure them; not to the half of ourselves and the half of our posterity, but to the whole people—women as well as men.**"**
>
> —Susan B. Anthony

According to the study's authors, it was because women were consistently left out of the networks of growth capital finance and appeared to lack the contacts needed to break through.

Or, as one female venture capitalist put it, "There's a built-in male network that's existed for a long time in the venture community, as well as the entrepreneurial community, that takes people a long time to break into."

Through Astia, I met Janneke Niessen, cofounder of Improve Digital, who told me, "My business partner and I have been on the receiving end of bias from investors on more than one occasion. Consciously or not, most picture a successful entrepreneur as a young white man."

Make no mistake: if you are a female company founder, the deck is stacked against you. The focus on gender diversity in funding startups has gathered momentum in recent years, but it's still more of a philanthropic exercise than an economic imperative.

Sharon Vosmek, CEO of Astia, once said, "For women to succeed in high-growth startups, they need exactly what men need: access to a central and powerful network of experts and investors. Entrepreneurs are men and women; investors are men and women. All need a vibrant ecosystem that breaks across gendered business practices."

When the Diana Project conducted a new study from 2011–2013, it found that women had made some progress: Fully 15 percent of all VC-funded companies in that period had at least one female executive.[2] (Although, as we pointed out in Chapter 1, they receive only 2.19 percent of all funding.)

But here's the real kicker: In 2015, venture capital firm First Round analyzed ten years' worth of its investments into 600 founders across 300 companies.[3] Their top finding: Companies with at least one female founder performed 63 percent better than those with all-male founders.

Sixty-three percent!

While that's a win, here's another disheartening figure: The project found that businesses with even one woman on the executive team were four times less likely to receive funding.

Again, this bias isn't just against women; it's against anyone who "isn't like us." Or, as the authors of the study said, "Venture capital is heavily male and pale."

When Vivek Wadhwa ran into this "white wall" in the early 1990s—experiencing some of the same frustrations as his female counterparts in securing funding—he and other Indian entrepreneurs in Silicon Valley began meeting informally to help each other, eventually naming themselves TiE: The Indus Entrepreneurs.

They would critique each other's business plans, presentations, and pitches. They'd demo products to each other. They began swapping stories of different venture capitalists ("Oh, he's a real asshole—be ready for that," or, "This guy is open to working with people who aren't white—try him"). Eventually, they created a formal network, connected with more open-minded VCs, hired each other for their startups, and leveraged several individual wins for the good of Indian and other minority entrepreneurs.

The tribe survived where the individual had starved.

## Women-Focused VC Funding

Here is a quick roundup of VCs that are laser-focused on helping women make inroads as entrepreneurs:

- *37 Angels* (www.37angels.com/). NYC. Invests in about a dozen male-led or female-led startups. Seed money only.

- *500 Women* (https://500.co/500-women/). San Francisco. A part of 500 Startups. Backed 100-plus women-led companies. Committed to investing $100,000 in ten more.

- *Astia* (http://astia.org/). San Francisco. $14 million plus in 45 companies, from disaster management tech to mobile payments to consumer goods.

- *Belle Capital* (www.bellevc.com/). Minnesota. Early-stage investment in IT, life sciences, and clean tech. At least one female founder/C-suite exec and/or willing to recruit females to C-suite and BOD.

- *Broadway Angels* (www.broadway-angels.com/). San Francisco. Portfolio includes fintech, edtech, health care, fashion, and personal development investments, among others.

- *Built by Girls* (www.builtbygirls.com/). NYC. Early-stage. Mobile and consumer tech with at least one female founder. About 40 investments.

⚐ *Female Founders Fund* (http://femalefoundersfund.com/). NYC. Focused on NYC, LA, San Francisco. 30 investments. Ecommerce, web-enabled products and services.

⚐ *Golden Seeds* (www.goldenseeds.com/). NYC. $90 million plus in early-stage money in 85 companies from health care to finance.

⚐ *The JumpFund* (www.thejumpfund.com/). Tennessee. Focused on southeast U.S. More than a dozen investments from edtech to clean tech to manufacturing.

⚐ *Phenomenelle Angels Fund* (www.phenomenelleangels.com/). Wisconsin. Focused on women-owned and/or minority-owned or –managed businesses in Wisconsin and Midwest. IT, bio-tech, CPGs, and telecom.

⚐ *Pipeline Angels* (http://pipelineangels.com/). NYC. $2 million plus in 30-plus investments, from tech and fashion to health care and edtech.

⚐ *Plum Alley* (https://plumalley.co/). NYC. Focused on gender-diverse and gender-balanced founding teams in diverse industries, from wearable tech to consumer goods.

⚐ *Sofia Fund* (http://sofiafund.com/). Minnesota. Tech-focused; women on leadership team who own equity.

⚐ *Springboard Enterprises* (https://sb.co/). NYC. Women-led tech companies. $7.8 billion raised. 650-plus companies invested in. 15 IPOs.

⚐ *StarVest Partners* (http://starvestpartners.com/). NYC. $400 million plus across 50-plus companies focused on SaaS, data, ecommerce, and digital marketing. Growth equity/late stage.

- *Valor Ventures* (http://valor.vc/). Atlanta. Prefers East Coast. Woman and/or minority on founding team should have more than 10 percent equity.

- *Women's Venture Capital Fund* (www.womensvcfund.com/). West Coast. Diverse investments in fashion, edtech, interior design, smart data, mobile apps, and more.

## ~~It's Who You Know~~ Who Knows You?

You know the old saying "It's not about what you know, it's about who you know"? If only it were that easy. To succeed in high-stakes business, the real differentiator is who knows you. And that, my friend, requires you to build relationships while building your brand.

We're talking about networking.

Not the "let's go eat crappy finger food and hand out business cards at a local networking event" kind, but strategic networking: searching for, identifying, and investing in long-term relationships.

Women need skills and personal capital, but social capital is more important. We need help from below us, beside us, and above us. Everyone needs help, but few women understand how truly important relationships are. We don't live in a meritocratic world; never have and never will. We do live in a world where word-of-mouth is still the most powerful referral tool.

In PricewaterhouseCoopers' 2016 "Women in the Workplace" report we referenced earlier, the study found that men were more networked with other men than women were. That may be obvious, but they worked out the math:

- Men: 37 percent networked mostly with other men; 9 percent, mostly women; 55 percent, equal split

✈ Women: 27 percent networked mostly with other women; 27 percent, mostly men; 45 percent, equal split

Because the upper echelons of organizations are overwhelmingly male, this means that fewer women are networked with the people who can introduce them into these arenas.

While it may seem self-explanatory, this concept of strategic networking is profoundly important for women.

Those successful VC-funded startups that land billions of dollars in capital? As I hope I've demonstrated, their social networks play a huge part in getting financed. Those CEOs and new appointees to the board of directors? Friends of friends. Good ol' boys network.

In fact, a 2016 study from the *American Economic Review* found that a woman more than doubles her chances of serving on a publicly traded company in Singapore if she plays golf.[4]

I don't ascribe to the conspiracy theories that there are a handful of people controlling the world. This isn't planned. It just naturally happens. While boards of directors may employ headhunters to find qualified candidates for board seats or executive positions, the roles are still often given to someone recommended by some stakeholder of the organization. At the very least, the candidate is often vouched for by "a friend of a friend."

## How Does Your Boardroom Grow?

PricewaterhouseCoopers' 2016 "Annual Corporate Directors Survey" confirms something we all know: when a board begins to look for new directors, nine out of ten times, candidates come from board members' recommendations.

However, the survey shows some progress. Boards are listening to investor recommendations more (well, slightly more), and 11 percent now search public databases to find potential board members.

My observation is that nearly all board seats are filled from, or at the very least influenced by, referrals. Networking is everything. Women and minorities aren't part of the dominant corporate culture, so they start on the outside and have to eventually work their way in.

Or, like Vivek, bypass it altogether.

## Try the New Way to "Network"

As I said earlier, I can't tell you how many impressive, accomplished, high-ranking women I've talked to, mentored, or coached who admitted they have impostor syndrome: They feel like a fraud and live in almost constant fear that someone will expose them.

As we discussed in Chapter 4, this isn't healthy—but it is normal. Unfortunately, these feelings of inadequacy can lead you to feel as though you have to make it on your own. You don't.

What do our rule breakers do to achieve the success they want? They create their own networks of like-minded people who are committed to mutual support—not the transactional what-can-you-do-for-me-now type of networking we usually see.

I cringe when I get an email from a complete stranger that says, "Hey, I see you're an accredited investor. Invest in my business!" No introduction, no references, no relationship. And every one of them is male. While I applaud the blind reach-out, it doesn't work with me. I invest with my heart as well as my gut. I believe in networking for new opportunities because only investing in my circle would perpetuate the problem, not fix it. And besides, those kind of transactional reachouts do not represent the kind of networking we're talking about.

In talking about gaining access to be invited to be on a board of directors, one of my research interviewees said, "Networking is the time you commit to developing a business-personal relationship with someone. . . . It's a mutual commitment between two people who develop this relationship that has no immediate benefit." In fact, most of the women who do this don't even think of it as networking. It's just about having relationships.

In *Stiletto Network*, author Pamela Ryckman profiled women-focused groups springing up across the globe. What Pamela noted was how intimate these groups were. In addition to discussing business, they talk about their fears in life and work and create genuine friendships. Instead of putting on the masculine facade women are told to assume, they are comfortable in their own form of femininity. In addition, they were incredibly open and willing to connect Pamela with others who, in turn, introduced her to yet still more (leading to the book itself).

What I love about Pamela's examples is that these women aren't focused exclusively on helping each other climb the corporate ladder but on mutually supporting each other's goals, whatever those happen to be.

That comes back to the central theme of this book: Success isn't necessarily about becoming a CEO or getting on the board of directors. It's about identifying a life that works for you, figuring out a lifestyle that fits those goals, and then finding the help you need to achieve that.

In her Billboard's Woman of the Year acceptance speech, Madonna said, "As women, we have to start appreciating our own worth and each other's worth. Seek out strong women to befriend, to align yourself with, to learn from, to collaborate with, to be inspired by, to support, and enlightened by."

Women must define their own path to success. Once they do, they can identify others who share a similar life vision. Then they can form a network of like spirits to help each other reach their goals.

## Name Your Tribe

Pamela Ryckman's *Stiletto Network* is a wonderful book that showcases our tribes: how they come together, how they work, and how they're changing the world.

When you find and form your tribe, you will need a great name. Here are some of the best I've found, culled from *Stiletto Network*, my networks, and a few other sources:

## disrupters

- 4C2B (as in, "to be reckoned with")
- Alley to the Valley
- Babes in Boyland
- Chicks in Charge
- ChIPs (Chiefs in IP)
- Girls Raising
- Harpies
- Ladies Who Latte
- Lady Business
- New Girls' Network
- Power Puff Girls
- SLUTS (Successful Ladies Under Tremendous Stress)
- Sphinxx
- The Harem
- The Little Black Dress Group
- The Pink Tank
- The Wafia
- VIEW (Very Important Executive Women)
- WiNGs (Women's Network Group)
- Women 2.0
- WOW (Women of Wisdom)

## Forget Networks—Focus on Relationships

Like mentoring programs and diversity initiatives, women's leadership and/or networking associations usually fail to deliver on their promise.

I've never found a woman yet who sincerely enjoyed going to networking events. Who really likes holding a glass of cheap chardonnay while exchanging business cards and superficial niceties? Thankfully, we can stop. The empirical and anecdotal evidence says it just doesn't help. In fact, not one of my dissertation subjects spent time pursuing this kind of networking.

What does help is finding women with whom you can have genuine relationships—women who will support you, advise you, encourage you, advocate for you, and go to bat for you. (Again, *Stiletto Network* does a fabulous job showing all the different forms that's taking across the world.)

Our wonder women don't just network inside their industry. They purposely cultivate a network that spans multiple industries. When one executive, formerly the CEO of a software company, sought to be on the board of directors of another company, she looked outside IT. "I want to keep learning. I could be valuable to a software company, but I want to move out of my comfort zone. That's really the only way you grow," she told me.

## My Imaginary Foe

One of my best mentors was a man in the C-suite of a Fortune 500 company. He was the one person who called me out for making decisions out of fear, forever changing the way I saw myself and looked at opportunities. I will be eternally grateful to him for helping me find my competence, probably the most important muscle in my current leadership arsenal.

I also hated him.

When I first met him, he came off as nice—too nice. He was a charis-
matic rising star and the smartest guy in the room. I didn't trust him.

As he moved up the ranks, I found a group of people who shared a
mutual dislike of the guy. The only time our team interacted with his
was when our departments overlapped: when they thought work we
were doing was theirs and vice versa. They were typical land-grab,
"building my kingdom" type battles. If people have archenemies,
he became mine.

As his responsibilities grew, so did his influence within the company.
He was no longer a rising star; he was a shining star. But the more
brightly he shined, the more it frustrated those of us who knew what
he really was. He was an outsider who had swooped in, formed the
right alliances, and ridden the glass elevator to the top. Of course,
there was so much more to his story. So much hard work. So much
putting himself out there with new ideas and new ways of doing
things. I didn't see it then.

The whole time I was sitting around with the mutual dislike club,
deep down I knew something was wrong. I preached a culture of
inclusion, but that stopped as soon as I met a person I didn't like. It
was a bitterness poisoning my soul.

Fast-forward a few years, and my then-boss of a month called me
on the phone and told me the company was reorganizing. You know
how those conversations go: "Thank you for your service. Here's
your pink slip. Your last check will be ready in two weeks. HR is on
the phone. Goodbye and good luck!"

I didn't take it personally. These kinds of restructurings happen all
the time: An executive decides the company needs to downsize a

division and gives his managers a quota to cut without respect to merit or length of service.

One of the first people I called was my archnemesis. To this day, I don't know why. Maybe I was just desperate. Maybe deep down, I knew I'd pegged him wrong. Maybe it was a strange manifestation of guilt.

Would you believe he called me back immediately? Not to gloat, but to help. Despite his by-then-enormous responsibilities, he patiently listened to my professional and personal woes and my desire to stay with the company even if my department was dissolving. He didn't just offer to help. He told me he would gladly hire me and that I could define what I wanted to do for him.

It did bolster my confidence that within two days, I had 20 offers from other departments and companies when they found out I was being let go. But I decided to go work for my former foe and even asked him to become my mentor.

When I had established enough of a relationship to own up to my mistrust and misdeeds, I discovered he was completely unaware of my feelings. He'd never been my enemy. I'd made the whole thing up in my head!

This isn't an episode I'm proud of. In fact, I'm embarrassed to share this in a book. But it's important that I hold the mirror up to myself. It's important to remember that change begins with me. And it's important to be grateful for forgiveness and goodness in those who support us and teach us lessons.

This isn't a call to create a sexist "no boys allowed" club. More often than not, the strategic relationships of our heroines include men (like Vivek, recognized by the *Financial Times* in 2015 as "one of ten men worth emulating in his support of women"). Ideally, a network comprises a healthy representation of not just both genders but a cross section of people from diverse industries, backgrounds, skill sets, positions, ethnicities, and more.

There are many men who do get it, who use their voices and their checkbooks to level the playing field. Among the enlightened who don't just talk but also act are founder of investment firm Lucas Point Ventures Adam Quinton, investor Brad Feld, Canadian Prime Minister Justin Trudeau, Berkshire Hathaway's Warren Buffett, Microsoft

## Men: We Need Your Help

To see real change in workplace gender equity, we need male allies.

Research from Rice University shows that men respond more positively to articles on gender equality when attributed to a male author.[5] The same articles, when attributed to female authors, weren't received as well. In other words, men need to hear it from other men.

This speaks to what Pat Milligan refers to in Chapter 10 as top executives taking on gender equity as a personal mission. When men see other men personally and sincerely advocating on behalf of gender diversity and inclusion, it challenges their own stance. If you happen to be in a position of power and can implement the policies and technologies we've discussed in this book, that's great. Regardless of your role and responsibilities, though, you can still be an ally for gender equity. You have influence simply by virtue of being a man.

*Reinforce women.* In a meeting, on a conference call, or elsewhere, when a woman makes a good point, publicly recognize it, repeat it, or positively address it: "Bethanie, I think you're right. If we built on that idea . . ." If a woman makes a point that goes unnoticed but is then picked up by a man as if he just came up with it, give credit to the woman: "Yeah, I think that's what Ann was saying just a minute ago when she said . . ." If someone interrupts a woman (especially to do some mansplaining), interject and hand the floor back to the woman: "Hang on, Ted, hang on—I don't believe Kate was finished with her point yet."

*Volunteer to be a mentor/sponsor.* This benefits you and the woman. It helps you become more aware of unique issues facing women and gets you more comfortable giving feedback to a woman. On the woman's part, not only does she benefit from having a mentor, but she also gets someone higher up in the company in her corner.

*Know the numbers.* When you know the facts, you can make the business case for gender equity. You can point out exactly how much pay disparity hurts the bottom line. You can pull out statistics on the real reasons women are leaving the company. You can demonstrate the ineffectiveness of most diversity initiatives.

*Champion women.* As we've discussed, one of the reasons women don't get recognized for promotions and other opportunities is because they don't have anyone championing them at the top. In volunteering to be a mentor/sponsor, you'll naturally champion the women you help. But beyond championing those women, champion women in general. Talk about gender equity. Talk about diversity. Be an advocate for women, especially when there are no women in the room. This makes it OK for the rest of the people in the room to do the same.

founder Bill Gates, and SAP CEO Bill McDermott. These men value what women bring to the table. They talk the talk and walk the walk.

Cultivating relationships is an ongoing process. One woman told me, "You know, I keep running into this former comptroller of a large company. She has the same skills I do, but she's only on one board. When she says how much she'd like to get on another, I ask, 'How much networking are you doing?' She says, 'Oh, I haven't really got to it yet.' And I think, *Well, it doesn't happen magically.*"

It's not magic. It's work.

> **"**What I am wearing doesn't matter. It never has. What matters is bringing forward disruptive ideas informed by data. That conversation is not about imbalanced power plays. We are all on the same side, working toward the same direction.**"**
>
> —Stephanie Buscemi

# the power of the tribe

Miriam Christof started one of the first formal tribes—if you can ever call a tribe "formal"—that I became part of. Just about every female executive in the Boston tech scene knows Miriam, even though she's now back in her native Germany. (Even continents and oceans apart, that's how close-knit our tribe is.)

As a principal and founder at JustJump Marketing, she's an expert on international marketing and especially digital media. But I suspect her legacy will be felt more in how she helps people connect with each other.

### How did your tribe come to be?

Eight years ago, I moved to Boston, and I didn't know anybody.

In the adventure with my own company, I attended a lot of networking events and became part of many organizations. These events were hosted and filled by a wide variety of people. All of them do really important work in connecting people, but I was looking for something that would allow me to make a deeper connection with select people interested in tangible results.

That is the difference between the tribe and a networking group. It is a trusted band of people who all have one thing in common. We are at a high level in our career, or just at the edge of that point, where we have achieved success but we really want to make a difference. In a tribe, you look to change things, to help each other with job placements, with the next gig, with support, and with all the other things that we can't always get from our wider networks of friends, family, colleagues, and acquaintances. Being part of our tribe allows us to create relationships that are enormously valuable in our careers.

We also have a very strong personal connection. We have people who get along with each other. They have complementary characters. What makes us so proud, though, is when we hear women saying the tribe is a safe haven for them. It's a place where you can talk about the things you normally wouldn't in a professional setting.

### *Without betraying any confidences, what does that look like?*

When you are a woman in a high-level position, say a C-level position, and you are thinking about a career change, that's difficult to do. You cannot tell a lot of people for fear of jeopardizing your current position. You have to be quite careful how you approach that.

But you can talk to people in our tribe—maybe in one-on-one conversations or sitting next to someone at the table—and immediately they will start charting a potential course for you. They will reach out to their own networks and within the tribe itself, introducing you, saying, "Hey, let me connect you to this person," and you know that the conversations will be kept in confidence.

You can also talk about business problems that you're struggling with. Some of us are entrepreneurs, and, like every business owner, we have business problems: "Our pipeline is dry" or "We're having a real problem delivering quality to our clients" or "We're going through a hard time with our cash flow."

You could never say these things in a strategic networking group because you have a reputation to keep up. These are the challenges every business goes through, but you cannot admit those things out loud because of the fear of how your stakeholders will react.

But in the tribe, you can do that without being judged. It is a judgment-free zone. Instead, the tribe jumps in to help. They immediately ask, "How can I help this person? Can I make an introduction? What would be valuable to them right now?"

You share the same fears and problems as you would with your closest friends and family. The problem with our friends and family is that often they're not in the same profession or at the same level of responsibility as you are. If one of your friends is a schoolteacher, she cannot help you find your next CFO, right? Your parents may want to give you advice about a workplace issue, but they have no context.

So the tribe is the intersection of women at similar levels in their careers who can offer help and advice, as well as a group of friends you can go have a drink with.

It's not like we hang out every weekend. We may come together every two or three months, but in between we're emailing, meeting up one-on-one or in small groups, jumping on a quick conference call, or just calling to keep up the relationship.

*It's not a networking group, it's not a support group, and it's not a referral group, is it? It's so much more.*

I think of it as an intentional power network. If you want to make it sound more touchy-feely, you could say "power network with a heart." You have those power networks all over where super-powerful women come together to really focus on career advancement, but I think our tribe focuses on the personal side, too.

We're intentional in who we invite into the tribe. We're mindful of how adding them influences the vibe we have. Our effectiveness as a band of sisters has a lot to do with finding people who fit into the group, on a personal level and a professional level.

We do not invite junior associates, for example, not because we don't love them, but because our tribe is not the right place for them. We invite women who have achieved a certain success in their career or are high-growth entrepreneurs. We want women who can make things happen. While junior people are awesome and will be the next generation of tribes, that's not the purpose of our tribe.

### How did the tribe come about?

In the beginning, we started with a small, formal group of six to eight business owners and business leaders focused on solving business problems. It was a structured environment where you could talk about the problems of your business. When that think tank—it was actually called the Pink Tank, funnily enough—ended after three years, Nicole [Sahin, founder of Globalization Partners] and I said, "There's something here."

When you go out to a networking event or to a conference, everybody has those people you enjoy talking to and feel comfortable around. If you can find three or four of those people, that's all you need to start with. You don't need a huge tribe.

Our tribe was small for quite some time. Then we decided that there were so many amazing women in Boston who didn't know each other. So we slowly opened our group up to people we trusted. Nicole and I set certain standards—really, without even talking about it. It was just a question of who would be a good fit? What caliber of person did we want to invite? We watched people at events and how they interacted with members of our tribe. Afterward, Nicole and I would talk to each other: "Hmmm, are they really the right fit? Have we seen them in action with others?" The biggest value our tribe has for its members is this personal connection above and beyond the professional benefit. That's what makes the tribe so powerful.

*How does the idea of the tribe tie into your vision of being a disrupter?*

When I think of disruption, the guiding question for me is, What's next? What else is possible? What else do I want to do? What could my next level of evolution as a leader look like in the company or as someone who's achieved some standing within the business community? What's my next step?

When we started JustJump Marketing, we were working with a lot of small businesses. My now-business partner came onboard, and the immediate question for us was "What's next?" What else do we want to do?

We started moving away from small businesses and toward midmarket companies to work with them on strategy. That's where we see our superpower as a company: helping organizations build marketing machines that intersect marketing strategy, process, and technology.

For me, I didn't know anybody when I first came to Boston, but I had a very clear idea of who I wanted to be in three years. I never wanted to be one of those people of whom people said, "Oh, she's a great deal-maker. She can close a million dollars in sales!"

I wanted to be somebody where people would say, "You know, I had lunch with Miriam, and it was just wonderful because she helped me do this."

I wanted to be a professional with a purpose beyond just the transaction. I wanted to be connected to the women in my tribe because I really believe we can disrupt the status quo when it comes to female leadership. If we form more of these tribes, we can push each other in a good way and open more opportunities for each other.

The tribe supports the evolution of the female leader, and these leaders are disrupting their companies, their industries, and their communities. The tribe helps her open doors without her always having to push those doors open on her own.

### So you like the title Disrupters?

I love it.

I don't want to accept the status quo just because it's the status quo, nor do I want to change the status quo just for the sake of change. When you disrupt something, you want to disrupt it for the better. When you identify a situation where you say, "You know, the status quo is good, but if we look at it like this, we can create something better for the company/person/ technology in this space."

That's what disruption is to me. I think it's overused today. Everybody's disrupting everything. "I'm disrupting the coffee industry by introducing a new bean!" That's not disruption.

I saw a commercial the other day saying this bank was disrupting banking because you didn't need your bank card to get money out of the ATM anymore—you can just use your cell phone. That's not changing the status quo.

Here's a small example of a disruptive idea. I have a different perspective on networking because it's practiced differently in Europe than in the United States. In the U.S., networking is often events hosted by men and filled with men, with people acting extremely interested in whatever you do. Often, they're just being polite: They enthusiastically ask about your business and take your card. They say, "This is awesome! Yes, I definitely want to talk about this, this is great!" but they don't have any real intention of furthering that relationship. Again, they're being polite, but the connection lacks substance.

In Europe—and especially in Germany—they only give you their business card if they really are interested in continuing the conversation. Networking is tough. But it's also a very honest reaction. I'm not saying that one is necessarily better than the other. I'm just saying there is a lot more "noise" in the way we network in the United States.

But most of the real networking doesn't take place at networking events. These are quite shallow in terms of relationship building. The real conversations take place in informal discussions, through relationships built over time, on the golf course, or these other places that are often invisible or inaccessible to women. There are real limits to what traditional networking can do. If someone introduced this different kind of networking to the U.S., it would disrupt our whole approach to the activity.

Disruption is looking at how things are currently done and seeing that it could be better. It's also about taking action. If you think networking could be done better but you let fear hold you back, then disruption cannot take place. If you think that people would judge you for trying something new or that if you created a tribe you'd be surrounded by a lot of bitching—if you let fear hold you back, you will never be able to truly disrupt things and create something better.

*In describing JustJump, you used the word "superpower."*

I used it in the context of our company, but I think everyone needs to discover their own superpower as individuals, too. Many women haven't identified that yet, but it's really important. They underestimate or undervalue something they do really well.

For me, being a power connector is my superpower. I deeply care about people, but that did not turn into my superpower until I decided there should be another way to network. Once I started doing that, my deep concern about people and the connections I made turned into something I could use strategically.

In the beginning, I didn't talk too much to the power players in Boston because I thought I had nothing to bring to the table, that I had nothing to say. I figured out after a while that the opposite was true. I really enjoyed our conversations, so over time I was able to create this network. Now, people say, "Wow, if you need an introduction to this person, reach out to Miriam because she knows everybody!" That's not true, of course. No, I don't know everybody. But the reason I know the people I do is because I stopped allowing the fear of rejection to hold me back from pursuing my superpower.

But having a superpower does not mean you're a superhero. You have to give yourself the benefit of the doubt sometimes. If you don't let your fear hold you back and go for it, but after some time you realize it's not working out the way you thought it would, then the question becomes, "What else could I do to achieve my goal?" If it doesn't work out, it's not the end of your story. It's important to keep going.

Get out there. Be courageous. Be fearless.

↗ ↗ ↗

Seth Godin popularized the word "tribe," but his concept is more akin to people sharing an affinity around an idea, a movement, or a brand. As you can tell from my conversation with Miriam, for us, a tribe is a beautiful, unique blend of personal and professional relationships.

These relationships don't take the place of our other friendships, of course. They're not a proxy for relationships with our extended family. They don't replace colleagues and peers with whom we have strictly collegial interactions.

It's a similar sentiment to what John D. Rockefeller said: "A friendship founded on business is a good deal better than a business founded on friendship." These are professional relationships that grow and blossom in sisterhood.

It's important to focus on the intentionality of Miriam and her co-tribal leader, Nicole. Every member of the tribe shares that same intention; it is the glue that connects us. The women in our tribe aren't just other professional women that we happen to love; rather, they are all peers. As Miriam said, we've reached a comparable level of professional achievement. The help we give each other feels reciprocal. Almost all of us coach, mentor, advise, and otherwise help other women, but our tribe is our sacred haven.

lead like a woman

*". . . I don't go by a rule book . . . I lead from the heart, not the head."*

—Princess Diana

From 2012 to 2015, Boston-based Globalization Partners grew an astonishing *16,000* percent, with no venture capital or angel investors. From zero to more than $17 million in annual revenue.

The company helps U.S. businesses expand internationally by cutting employee acquisition time from six months (or even a year) down to as little as three days. Talk about a major game changer! This company is redefining—no, revolutionizing—an entire market.

Theirs is an incredible story about how to create something from nothing, how to manage meteoric growth, and how to land in the top ten of the Inc. 500 list of fastest-growing companies. When they made the list, what was the media hype all about?

Their gender.

"If we were an all-male founding team, no one would mention it," founder and CEO Nicole Sahin told me.

But because the leadership team was all-female, Globalization Partners almost became a circus attraction: "Step right up! You won't believe what this company looks like! You've never seen anything like it! Tickets only five bucks!"

While I'm all for celebrating women's wins, the media missed the deeper, more revelatory story behind Globalization Partners. The company is run by women, but its leadership tries to embody both male and female traits—"androgynous leadership," if you will.

Welcome to the future. And before you jump to any conclusions, as part of the company's growth strategy, HR is focused on creating a more gender-balanced, inclusive work force with a target of a 50–50 ratio.

## Traditional Leadership Doesn't Work Anymore

Henry Ford's melting pot approach worked because he lived in the Industrial Age. Competitive advantage centered on achieving economies of scale, like Ford's River Rouge factory. With nearly 16 million square feet of factory floor, 100 miles of railroad *inside* the facility, and 100,000 employees at its peak, it was by far the largest industrial complex in the world.

Such massive manufacturing processes required a command-and-control approach to business: centralized decision making, a military-like hierarchy, and strict adherence to policies and procedures to keep things humming along.

From the outside, titans of industry like Henry Ford, Andrew Carnegie, J.D. Rockefeller, and Cornelius Vanderbilt led progress. From the inside, though, they weren't leaders; they were authoritarians. Unfortunately, their style of "leadership" became the model. The

> ## Get in Touch with Your Feminine Side
>
> Introverts, the analytical, and peacemakers are finding more success by creating a leadership style that's true to their own nature, rather than trying to copy the "great man" style of leading. Consultants, leadership experts, and life coaches are advising men to embrace their natural tendencies, use their personality traits as strengths, and rely more on their intuition and feelings to guide them. In other words, men are being told to let their female leadership traits shine. Finally!

structures and culture of that age cemented themselves not as *a* way to do business, but *the* way.

Shortly thereafter, experts like economist Milton Friedman came along and decreed that the stockholder theory was the only rational approach to business. That is, the sole purpose of a company is to maximize profit for its shareholders.

Now that we live in the Digital Age, where economies of scale and massive industrialization count for almost zilch, this antiquated approach to management is strangling companies.

Unfortunately for all of us, this is how men were socialized to lead.

## The "Great Man" Model

In the game King of the Hill, one kid climbs, claws, and scratches his way to the top of the slide, jungle gym, haystack, or literal hill. Once he takes the high ground, he fends off everyone else as they try to claim his crown. There's only one winner; everyone else loses.

This is the way men generally approach business. It's a winner-take-all, "kill the competition" death match—both inside and outside the company. They want to dominate the market, eliminate their rivals, and rise to the top of the pack.

In *The Art of the Start*, Guy Kawasaki advises would-be entrepreneurs to show their business plans to a few women. If they don't think it makes sense, scrap the idea. His theory is that men have an evolutionary "killer gene" that makes them perceive things more aggressively and competitively than women—even with something as abstract as a startup.

Men may make great pioneers and trailblazers, but that doesn't automatically make them great leaders. Leadership used to be understood as the ability to take charge: to project confidence, to make swift decisions, to be courageous, to be steadfast in the face of danger.

In other words, leaders looked like lone warriors.

Our culture, from our origin beliefs to fairy tales to modern media, espouses the idea of a "great man." The lone heroes in our stories wade into danger, slay the dragon, and conquer the wilderness. Odysseus. Andrew Carnegie. King Arthur. Thomas Edison. Batman. Steve Jobs. Jesus.

When we talk about their exploits, the tales often focus on the hero, their challenges, and their courageous choices. They look within themselves to find the answers, make the hard choice, and forge ahead. Hail the conquering hero.

Except that idealized version is a myth, even in the myths. None of these real or imaginary men accomplished great things all on their own. There's no such thing as the lone hero. Every person who reached the top had help getting there. Odysseus had the help of Athena. Andrew Carnegie got his start as an inside man for railroad profiteers. King Arthur had his Knights of the Round Table. Edison relied on "the Boys" running the experiments at Menlo Park. Where would Batman be without Alfred? Steve Jobs started Apple with Steve Wozniak. Jesus had the Twelve Disciples.

Heck, even the Lone Ranger had Tonto.

This persistent myth still informs the way we think about leaders. We hold these lone wolves up as the ideal to which we should aspire. But these archetypes discourage people in general from admitting their inabilities and shortcomings . . . and do so even more for women and minorities, since they have something to prove over and above their white male colleagues.

# Wonder Woman

As I like to do, let's talk numbers.

As of this writing, the 2017 movie *Wonder Woman*:

- Grossed more than $820 million worldwide
- Highest-grossing film with a solo female director
- Largest U.S. opening of a film with a solo female director
- Largest opening for a female-led comic book movie
- One of the best-rated superhero movies ever, coming just behind *The Dark Knight* and *Iron Man*

Yes, it's amazing. Yes, I've seen it twice already. Yes, it is the super-heroine movie we need.

*Wonder Woman* needed to overcome the dismal failures of the last two female solo superhero movies: *Catwoman* with Halle Berry and *Elektra* with Jennifer Garner. There have also been a scant few movies directed by women, with extra scrutiny on those few.

In *Wonder Woman*, though, it seems studio execs had a novel idea: what if they cast a solo female superhero film with—wait for it—a female director!

Director Patty Jenkins did an amazing job. Women came out of the theater ready to take on the world. Actress Gal Gadot embodied a woman's idea of a superheroine.

Why did we love it so much? What was it about *Wonder Woman* that struck such a chord? I think a Tumblr user (username: Creative Words, Powerful Ideas) said it best:

> Watching a superhero movie directed by a woman is like putting glasses on for the first time.

I didn't realize how much I had to squint through the "male gaze" till suddenly, miraculously, I didn't have to. There were absolutely NO eye candy shots of Diana. There were Amazons with aging skin and crow's-feet and not ONE of them wore armor that was a glorified corset. When Diana did the superhero landing, her thigh jiggled on-screen.

Did you hear me? HER FUCKING THIGH JIGGLED. Wonder Woman's thigh jiggled on a 20-foot-tall screen in front of everyone.

Because she wasn't there to make men drool. She wasn't there to be sexy and alluring and flirt her way to victory, and that means she has big, muscular thighs, and when they absorb the impact of a super-hero landing, they jiggle. And. That's. WONDERFUL.

Thank you, Patty Jenkins, for giving me a movie about a woman, told by a woman, so I can see it through my eyes, not some dude bro who's there for boobs and butt.

*mic drop*

By continuing to acquiesce to this model of how we should be, we're not creating realistic aspirations for workers in the Digital Age. The gunslinging cowboy who rushes into a hail of bullets isn't the person you want as a project team lead.

Reality is too complex for any one individual to handle alone. We need people who can collaborate, innovate, communicate, anticipate, adapt, react, and pivot. Effective leadership in the modern age doesn't revolve around who can make the most decisions or even the best decisions. Today's leaders are those who can affect the most positive change.

## The Way Women Lead

Unfortunately, that's not the culture most people live in. We usually find ourselves in Stephanie Buscemi's shoes, the Salesforce executive vice president we met earlier. As I related, she's a successful executive in an overwhelmingly male-dominated, engineering-focused tech company. Most women in the workplace—and especially someone in Stephanie's position—have been directed to lead like a man. That meant a command-and-control approach, emphasizing assertive decision making, a rational (read: emotionless) approach, and a stockholder-centric approach to business.

Stephanie said, "This isn't going to work for me or anyone else," and decided to lead her own way. She eschewed how she was "supposed to lead" and created a leadership style that was genuine, natural, and—perhaps most important—more effective *for her and her team*.

By this point, I hope you've realized that, to achieve the life you want and the success you crave:

- You don't have to aspire like a man.
- You don't have to dress like a man.
- You don't have to act like a man.

You don't. You don't have to throw yourself into Henry Ford's melting pot and come out as another assimilated corporate employee, ready to be part of the mothership.

What we've been doing over the course of this book is rediscovering your instincts, your passions, and your intuition. If you haven't been giving yourself permission to be who you are, I hope this book is encouraging you to do so.

Finally, I want you to realize that you don't have to lead like a man.

In 1958, Lawrence Kohlberg finished his dissertation on what came to be known as "Kohlberg's stages of moral development." It was quite a pioneering move, since psychology still wasn't regarded as a serious science, and morality was considered a subjective topic. (How can you quantify how moral an individual is?) Nevertheless, Kohlberg pursued his research and eventually came to be recognized as one of the pre-eminent psychologists in history.

Of course, like any academic, he had his critics. Perhaps his earliest was his own research assistant, Carol Gilligan, who became a distinguished psychologist in her own right. Gilligan thought Kohlberg's research was too narrow: he focused almost exclusively on how men made decisions and looked for the patterns in their moral development. Gilligan, on the other hand, didn't believe that women's morality mirrored men's; she thought they had a fundamentally different rationale for how they viewed ethical behavior and weighed decisions.

To her credit, Gilligan didn't believe that one was superior to the other. She said there were two "voices," a masculine and a feminine, and that ideally a person would listen to both to realize their full potential in moral development.

> **"** *A strong woman understands that the gifts such as logic, decisiveness, and strength are just as feminine as intuition and emotional connection. She values and uses all of her gifts.* **"**
>
> —Nancy Rathburn

Carol Gilligan's work influenced my early research into gender equity, and I wholeheartedly agree with her major point: it takes both perspectives. This is precisely why Nicole Sahin's team at Globalization Partners follows an androgynous approach to leadership. By blending the two, they've created a company culture that has made their incredible growth possible, while also allowing for a radically different lifestyle from most high-growth startups. The message is clear: You don't have to choose one leadership culture over another when both are needed.

So how do men and women lead differently?

## How We Make Great Decisions

If you've ever taken a business or economics course, you've had Milton Friedman's core principle pounded into your skull: The only reason to do anything in a company is to make as much money as possible for its owners.

I'm an angel investor, business owner, and public company shareholder. I know that a company has to turn a profit. But I'm not so narrow-minded as to believe that executives should pursue that goal to the exclusion of all else. I couldn't sleep at night knowing my teams, businesses, and investments were hurting people for a few extra cents. Just because you can use a sweatshop in China doesn't mean you should. Just because a foreign government doesn't restrict you from dumping toxic waste into its water supply doesn't mean it's a good idea.

What we're talking about is stockholder (aka shareholder) vs. stakeholder. When making major decisions, the masculine approach focuses on how the outcome affects the stockholders: the people who own the company, division, department, project, etc. It's a linear, hierarchical perspective.

The feminine approach looks at the stakeholder perspective: In addition to the people who "own" the results of this decision, who else will be affected? What other departments, companies, individuals, customers, and vendors will this decision impact? This is usually called a radial approach to decision making: looking not just up and down the organizational chart, but laterally and even outside it completely.

In Chapter 4, I talked about the CEO's husband who griped that his wife took forever to make decisions. Notice that he didn't complain about the quality of her decisions once she arrived at them, just that she didn't come to them fast enough.

Yes, it took her longer because she's a woman; she decides differently. Instead of just looking at how the decisions would affect the lines on the P&L statement, she took other groups into consideration: not just stockholders, but employees, contractors, customers, suppliers, partners, communities, and families.

## How We See Authority

Along the same lines, the masculine view of authority usually follows hierarchical structure: The person with the most authority is the one who has the most explicit authority, that is, the person with the biggest title.

Thus, when measuring their own power or influence, the masculine approach tends to view it in light of how much recognized authority they have. It's a factor in why formal titles and positions seem to be more important to men than women.

The feminine perspective tends to view authority in terms of implicit influence and reputation. A manager may be nominally in charge of an initiative but are they really the driver behind the project? Or is there someone lower on the totem pole who wields more influence over its direction?

(It reminds me of a cartoon I once saw that asked, "Do you want to speak to 'the man in charge' or the woman who knows what's going on?")

Thus, when we measure our own authority, we tend to think in terms of "platform": Have we cultivated relationships and a reputation that will enable us to move an initiative in the direction we want? It often bothers us less that someone else is nominally in charge so long as we're can achieve what we've set out to do.

## Why Our "Risk Lens" Looks Different

Masculine approach = pessimism

Feminine approach = realistic optimism

That reads like an oversimplification, and anyone can easily offer up examples of optimistic men and pessimistic women. But these descriptions aren't about personality types but about how the two gender traits generally approach business decisions.

For men, it's often the business version of King of the Hill: "The competition's climbing, so how do we get them before they get us? If we don't keep fighting, we'll lose. Stand your ground!" As a result, the masculine perspective sees risk as a chasm that could swallow everything they've gained but which must nevertheless be crossed.

Women tend to view business decisions more positively. Outcomes aren't "win/lose" but "better/best." Markets, customers, innovation, talent, and other resources aren't slices of pie where if mine's bigger, yours is smaller, but rather like water in the ocean: There is a finite supply, but it's so vast that it really doesn't matter. There's plenty to go around.

As such, women tend to view risk as an opportunity: not a chasm they might fall into but a roulette wheel where they have to spin to win—the gamble is a necessary part of the game.

# How a Woman Brought Down Blockbuster

*Lean In* author Sheryl Sandberg called it "the most important document ever to come out of the Valley." She was referring to "Netflix Culture: Freedom & Responsibility," a slide deck about corporate culture put out by Netflix's then-chief talent officer, Patty McCord.

The ideas in the document are radical, even for a Silicon Valley tech company. It's a unique mix of idealism and pragmatism, or what might be the love child of Mark Zuckerberg and Jack Welch.

You can't deny its results. Netflix went from a DVD-by-mail company whose main competitor used to be Redbox to the world's premier streaming service, as well as a film studio churning out high-quality content that's sent Hollywood scurrying and begun to redefine media consumption. (Oh, and bankrupted Blockbuster along the way.)

No, I can't lay the credit for disrupting the entire film industry at the feet of one woman. I can, however, point out that as one of the early executives of Netflix, and especially as its chief talent officer, she was an architect of disruption.

Business schools and MBA courses use Blockbuster as a cautionary tale and like to analyze how they could have avoided becoming obsolete. They approach business strategy from a high-level perspective.

But as one of my mentors and advocates, Jonathan Becher, former Chief Marketing Officer and Chief Digital Officer at SAP, constantly told his team, "Brick buildings don't do business with brick buildings. People do business with people."

Netflix didn't become the powerhouse it is today because CEO Reed Hastings did a SWOT analysis and identified a market need his company could fill. Netflix became Netflix because of its culture, and its culture comes from its people.

Why should you focus on gender equity? Why concern yourself with diversity and inclusion? Why worry about pay disparities? Because you don't want to become your industry's Blockbuster.

## Leadership: A Transaction or a Transformation?

In sum, the masculine approach is predominantly "transactional," while the feminine is predominantly "transformational."

You could call the former the carrot-and-stick approach. It's when you, as the authority figure, need your people to follow your and/or the organization's directives, so you give them clear goals and responsibilities, using a system of rewards and punishments to get them to comply.

Transformational leadership, on the other hand, emphasizes relationships, aligning personal values with organizational values, nurturing, mentoring, and giving people the tools they need.

I practice this. I want my teams to buy into what we're doing, to feel fulfilled, to have the tools they need, and to move forward confident that they have my support. When it comes to the overall goal, transformational leadership basically says, "I have a vision: Let me help you put your own footprint on this vision and align on common values and goals, so that you will not only achieve it with the larger group, but realize levels of collective success not thought possible by an individual." The job of a transformational leader is not to change people, but to give them the tools they need to change themselves and influence others.

The transformational approach sees working with others as collaborative, adaptive, and supportive. While the traditional model of management is task-oriented, transformational leaders take a more holistic view. Moreover, they often use a values-based approach: There isn't simply one way to lead. Values hold different meanings for different people. No one approach is any more correct than another, and my leadership style doesn't have to look like yours.

The transactional leader attempts to bring people into compliance. The transformational leader doesn't want to change people—they want to enable people to change themselves and, thereby, to effect change.

As complex and ever-changing as the marketplace is today, though, we have to take it one step further: generative leadership. This says, "I don't know what the vision should look like, so I'm going to enable you to create it with us." It recognizes the limitations of a single individual. It's almost like crowdsourcing a vision, albeit with a selective crowd.

## Understand What Drives the Genders

The women in my research study didn't feel the need to assert themselves as the alpha, yet they were clearly in charge. They saw their approach to leadership more in the role of a teacher or facilitator. They directed traffic, but they didn't necessarily have to be driving all the cars. They focused less on themselves and more on the purpose or shared vision of the group. They were less worried about social hierarchy and more concerned about whether they got something done. In other terms, their leadership style was less about ego and more about achievement.

This is nearly the polar opposite of the command-and-control approach the business world has been using since the dawn of the Industrial Revolution. It necessarily relinquishes centralized decision making, ceding authority to those closest to the situation.

There are pros and cons to each of these styles. One isn't necessarily better than the other. Different times and factors call for different approaches. The takeaway is that one size does not fit all. The feminine perspective offers a counterpoint to an all-male approach. We're not better; we're different.

# Follow the 16,197 Percent Growth Strategy

Now that we've seen the differences between men's and women's natural approaches to leadership, we can circle back to Nicole Sahin's all-female founding team and really understand how their androgynous approach to company culture resulted in growing the company from zero venture capital to more than $17 million in annual revenue and business in more than 150 countries in just three short years. Here are six strategies they used to drive their growth.

## An Inclusive Culture Doesn't Support the Company— It Drives It

Some feminists might celebrate the fact that women compose 75 percent of Globalization Partners' work force. Nicole actually wants that number to decrease to about 50 percent. This isn't some philosophical or moral question but a strategic goal. The company revolutionized its industry in part because its all-female founding team brought a radically different perspective to the marketplace. But those same women know that to stay innovative, they must continue to strive for a company comprising varied perspectives, experiences, and skill sets. Diversity doesn't do much, but inclusivity can be amazing.

When new hires come onboard, Nicole begins to build a personal relationship with them. Not only does she want to hear their ideas and gain fresh insights, and she wants them to feel that they're welcomed and a valuable addition to the overall fabric of the company. In short, she wants them to know that their diverse perspective isn't just permitted but expected.

## Purpose and Profit Go Hand in Hand

Globalization Partners is a professional employer organization: They help companies hire foreign employees quickly. But when I talked to the leadership team about *why* they do it, the conversation quickly switched from money to meaning. They felt they created and facilitated relationships across borders and boundaries.

Nicole said, "Through global commerce comes peace."

Echoing her sentiment, general counsel Nancy Cremins said, "It's hard to go to war against your teammate or someone you value who works for you."

It's not just about turning a profit or gaining market share, but about accomplishing something worthwhile while doing so.

## Think About It, Then Take the Risk

Despite being in the midst of that phenomenal growth, Nicole made the decision to stop taking new clients for several months.

For any high-growth startup, that's just unthinkable. But Globalization Partners' leadership team was concerned that the operations that led to their success might not be sustainable as they grew. They stopped taking on new business, continued to service their existing clients, and focused on building a structure for the future. It turned out to be the right choice.

This is a textbook example of what I spoke about earlier: Men see business barriers as obstacles, while women often see them as opportunities. Realizing they didn't have a scalable framework, the team allowed the challenge to become the catalyst they needed to step back, rework their business model, and then get back into the fray.

A male-dominated team would probably have followed the traditional high-growth startup approach: "Let's build the plane while we're flying it." The lack of scalable operations would simply have been a problem to fix, not an opportunity to take advantage of.

## Don't Hire an Employee; Hire a Person

Globalization Partners embraces the concept of whole life integration. They don't just deal with the person who shows up at the office but strive to offer a job that makes room for the rest of their employee's life. Flexible schedules, generous family leave, a smart re-entry program for new parents—this place is nirvana for women who want to succeed at life and business at the same time. In making business decisions, the executive team considers not just what's best for the company but also what works for the people who compose it.

## Invest in the Future by Investing in People

I almost fell off my chair when Nicole told me it's company policy to extend a paid sabbatical—including fully paid world travel—to employees after five years of service.

In case you didn't get that: They pay people to go see the world.

"Traveling around the world with my husband, meeting people who were so different from me, changed my life. I want my employees to be able to experience that too with their families," she explained.

## Executive Decisions Are Relational, Not Linear

Instead of *The Lean Startup*—inspired ethos of starting out as small and prototyping as quickly as possible, Nicole spent a year traveling the world to figure out Globalization Partners' business model.

Of course, not everyone can take a year off and be a jet-setter. That's not the point. She didn't create a minimally viable product, sell it, see what worked, and then pivot and iterate again. That is, she didn't start at point A, go to point B, and then hit point C.

Rather, she started outside herself. She talked to potential clients, providers, partners, and employees all over the world. She took multiple perspectives into account and then created a company that would work with all of them.

That kind of thinking—not "Where are we and where do we want to go?" but "What do our stakeholders need and how can we provide it?"—has made possible their fantastically profitable, fantastically fun journey.

By the time this book goes to print, Globalization Partners may have crashed and burned—many of the companies Jim Collins praised in *Built to Last* (published in 1994) and *Good to Great* (2001) now operate far south of greatness—but I promise it won't be because of these six strategic decisions. The way they operate is not just the male or female perspective but a beautiful blend of both.

# Realize It's Not About You

I once listened to an interview with comedian Jerry Seinfeld where the interviewer asked, "Why do you still do standup? You're *Jerry Seinfeld*.

It's not like you have to go back to the clubs. And you're often booed off stage. I mean, are you a glutton for punishment?"

Jerry answered (and I'm paraphrasing), "What are you talking about? They're not there to see me. They're there because they want to laugh."

In that moment, the light bulb went on. When I'm leading a group of people, *it's not about me*. It's about what it means to them. They're there for themselves; it's about *them*.

The corporate world tells us to go for consensus and alignment. That's going to kill us. Things move too fast and there are too many opportunities to seize for us to wait until we all get on the same page. Being able to fit every person into a neat little box isn't going to enable the next wave of innovation and value creation. Waiting until a manager can get a handle on a problem is a bottleneck approach that slows down progress and handicaps people. That's the opposite of what corporate executives say they need, yet they continue to use the same management style they've been using since the Industrial Revolution.

If they truly want to unleash creativity—if they want to create an ownership mentality, or an entrepreneurial approach, or whatever buzzword they happen to use—they simply need to create an environment that allows for more than one kind of leader.

Just get out of our way. We'll do the rest.

## Be the Leader You Want to Be

I subscribe to the postmodern view of leadership. Simply put: You do you, and I'll do me.

I'm a Boston-Irish descendant of an Armenian Genocide refugee, an investor in high-growth startups, a leadership futurist in the tech sector, an advocate for gender equity, the American wife of a wonderful English-South African husband, and the mother of two adorable daughters and a puppy.

Unless that also describes you—and I'd love to meet you if it does— what you hold near and dear to your heart will be vastly different from what I do. Your values, ideals, and worldview may coincide with some of mine, but most will correspond only occasionally. We may want the same general things (e.g., world peace, a cure for cancer, financial stability, a good night's sleep, the ability to eat whatever we want without gaining weight), but how we choose to pursue them will vary.

And that's OK.

By the time you and I had discussed all our differences and finally agreed on how to pursue our common goals, the world would have changed. The goals might not even make sense anymore. There's just no time to come to a consensus.

My concept of leadership doesn't focus on getting everybody to the same place, but rather on inspiring and equipping my followers to work toward the same vision. I believe I can lead change but only if my people:

- See me modeling the behavior, actions, and values I espouse (if I walk the talk)
- Are equipped with the skills and opportunities to act differently
- Have a compelling story; that they understand what's being asked of them and it makes sense
- Have the reinforcement they need to make those changes through the available structures, process, and systems

If they have that, together we can conquer mountains.

# explosive growth, a controlled burn, and a self-financed fortune

Yes, Nicole Sahin and her company, Globalization Partners, featured prominently in the previous chapter, but that description doesn't do justice to her achievements. So here's more about this amazing woman:

- Inc. 500's top-ten fastest-growing private companies 2016
- Inc. 500's number-one female CEO 2016
- EY's Entrepreneur of the Year 2017
- Went from $0 to $17 million in annual revenue in just four years—with zero outside investment

Yeah, Nicole kicks ass.

Here's the thing, though: On paper Nicole is incredible, but in everyday life, she really is like Wonder Woman. The goal of her global business is to tear down the barriers that divide us. She is the new face of leadership: one that combines decisiveness with inclusion and profit with conscience.

*Nicole, you came out of the high-growth world of the Silicon Valley and San Diego to found Globalization Partners in 2012, but in your first year, you didn't go the traditional high-growth route. Virtually every startup follows the "build the airplane while you're flying it" model, but you built the airplane first.*

Well, I can't say I wasn't doing a bit of flying while building, but let's say I at least had the wings and an engine!

In my first year, it was just me. I knew that I wanted to build a great company. For me, that meant achieving something great but also being a place that I loved to come to work. I needed to prove to myself that I had a viable business before I started involving other people's lives. When you bring an employee onboard, you're not just taking on the responsibility of payroll and providing space for them—you're asking them to leave their current job and join your company on nothing more than their faith in you. Before I could ask someone to take that risk, I had to know that this idea would work.

So my first year, I focused on working my network, landing some clients, creating the marketing and website, doing the paperwork, laying the operational foundation for the business by traveling to 24 countries, and just really laying the groundwork for my vision of a great business.

After a year, I finally realized how busy I was getting and had the confidence that the growth and momentum weren't going to stop any time in the foreseeable future. I also wanted to get ahead of the curve and hire someone before I absolutely needed them, so I brought on my first hire and then, a few months later, brought on my second.

*It is amazing that you hit $17 million in annual revenue inside four years without any outside investors.*

Thank you. I've worked with VC-backed companies, private equity, and other companies with investors. They're really hard on people. Especially in a services business, they're always pressing you to create an asset as quickly as you can instead of building a business. That's not the kind of culture I wanted for Globalization Partners.

To me, building the business of my dreams means having a triple bottom line. The shareholders need to be happy, but more importantly the clients need to be happy with what we're providing and the employees must be happy. If you're going to build a business that sustains itself over the long term, you need all the stakeholders satisfied and everyone aligned with how you've defined success. I mean, we're building bridges between cultures all over the planet. This is more than just a professional service: This is connecting people from around the world with the world's coolest companies. We're redefining how companies—and people—do business globally.

Instead of going the usual route of "Hey, I've got an idea—let's build a company around it and see if it works!" we went the other way: We built something to work and once it did, we built a company around that. We got solid revenue coming in the door, which I used for our first round of hires, then used the increased revenue to fuel the next group of hires, and then used that to fuel the next series of hires. That's allowed us to create the company we wanted without having to have external institutional investors.

### And what does Globalization Partners look like now?

We started the year with 40 employees and $18 million in revenue, with clients in hundreds of companies, but we've already grown one-and-a-half times just by the end of the second quarter. By the end of the year, we expect to have grown 300 percent: three times the clients, three times the employees, and three times the revenue.

### With zero external capital.

We get at least three or four investors calling or emailing every single day. I just don't even call them back anymore.

So many people think they need funding before they can do anything. If we were building spaceships or something capital-intensive, no, our model wouldn't work. But if you can build your business on cash flow and revenue, it gives you so much more freedom to run your company without outside interests potentially competing with your vision.

*It annoys me to no end that much of the media coverage on your company has been focused on the fact that you have an all-female executive team.*

It wasn't planned that way. I just did what most people do, I think: When I needed to hire someone, I looked at my network of people to see who was really good at scaling a business, what I needed in a particular role, and reached out to people. It just so happened that most of the incredibly talented people in my network were women.

The most important thing for me, though, was company culture. I'm not planning on selling this business anytime soon, and even when I do, I want to look back at my work and think not only of the dollars I earned but of the legacy I leave behind in people's hearts and minds. I do plan on being around for a long time. I want to hire people that I'm going to enjoy being around for all those years. I want to bring in people who are extremely collaborative, extremely powerful in terms of rolling up our sleeves and getting something done, and extremely effective at growing this business. I mean, this isn't a cupcake shop—we're building a legal platform on a global level.

*Cupcake shop?*

Women-founded and women-led businesses are typified. If someone says a woman's opening a business, plenty of people think cupcake shop or florist or something like that.

There's nothing wrong with opening a small business like that. My mother was a florist who worked incredibly hard, and my parents succeeded beyond their dreams by being small business owners. I respect anyone's worth and accomplishments at any level.

But Globalization Partners is a high-growth, tech-driven platform that delves into the legal realms of hundreds of companies. This is not an easy business, and especially not with the rapid growth we're experiencing. I say that spending a quarter year working with us is like spending a year working anywhere else because of how quickly things change. It's like extreme sports, but for business.

If you work with us, we will love you. You will love coming to work. We put a lot of effort into esprit de corps. At the same time, it is intense. We expect a lot out of every single person.

We have what we call "GP University" the first day you join the team. Part of it is where I charge them with the responsibility to not just enjoy our culture but to make sure they embody it and carry it forward, both in relationships with each other as well as in pursuing a high-performance culture of achievement.

### *Did you begin networking with recruitment in mind?*

Not at all. I just wanted to be around people I could connect with on both a personal and professional level. There were business problems that I wanted to get another perspective on, but I wanted to go into a deeper conversation than you can with most business acquaintances.

Really, I just wanted to surround myself with interesting people that I saw as change makers. Once I found them, I got intentional about spending more time with them. That's how Miriam [Christof], another Boston-based entrepreneur, and I formed our tribe. We're good friends who can help each other with professional problems.

The first time I needed some legal advice, I reached out to my tribe to ask who they'd recommend who would understand the unique challenges of our business. They just happened to recommend a woman. She was our outside counsel for a while—just like we outsourced our marketing to Miriam until we grew big enough to bring it in-house—and then she came onboard as our general counsel, then became our chief administrative officer. We used another person in the tribe as a consultant for a time; then she came onboard as our chief operating officer. These two women, Nancy Cremins and Debbie Millin, are fundamental drivers of our company and culture. I wouldn't want to be here without them.

So, no, I had no idea that I would find team members inside the tribe of women Miriam and I brought together. But it's wonderful. We started out as a group of friends and now get to work with each other every day creating something we're all proud of—a business that we love being part of.

⚑ ⚑ ⚑

Nicole is the poster child for *Disrupters*.

Not only is Globalization Partners disrupting the professional employer organization industry, but the way she went about building the company turns the whole high-growth business tech model on its head.

Most of the tech world has embraced Eric Ries' *Lean Startup* methodology. I like to think Nicole has pursued a woman's version of a lean startup. She tested the market and her business model first to ensure viability. Then she built the platform for a high-growth startup before bringing anyone else aboard because she was worried about the hypothetical lives of whoever her hires would be; she cared about her employees even when she didn't have any. She also feels that way about her customers.

What's more, regardless of how big Globalization Partners gets, she still sees the bigger mission: building bridges between people and countries. For her, business is an end unto itself . . . yet at the same time, it's a means to an end.

In Nicole Sahin, we see a beautiful balance of business pragmatism and personal idealism.

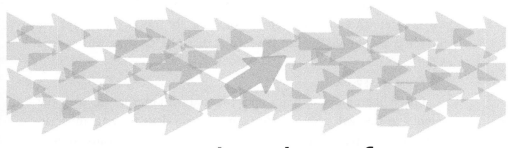

# open the door for someone else

*"There is a special place in hell for women who
don't help other women."*

—MADELEINE ALBRIGHT

D id you know ladies of the quiet sort possess the super-power of karma? Not asking for a raise is to your advantage. Your superiors will recognize your humility and your faith in their ability to allocate raises and promotions based on merit. Your efforts may not bear fruit in the short term, but in the long term you'll be rewarded for your good work.

For those of us who live and work on planet Earth, such a statement might be comical . . . were it not coming from the CEO of one of the world's largest companies.

Satya Nadella, CEO of Microsoft, gave that answer at the Grace Hopper Celebration of Women in Computing in 2014 when asked how women should approach negotiating for raises.[1] He said we shouldn't; we should instead have faith that HR systems will reward us fairly.

Trust the system.

That's like a judge telling a man charged with murder to "trust the system—justice will prevail." You could spend days reading about all the wrongly convicted innocents finally being released because of new evidence. "Oh, the system failed you. Sorry about that!"

A 2012 survey of chief financial officers at public companies in the U.S. found that, all other things being equal (company size, CFO experience, industry, etc.), the lower the CFO's pay, the more likely it was that they were a woman.[2] Further analysis showed that male CFOs' salaries are more than 16 percent higher than their female counterparts'. Even when they're making millions of dollars in the upper echelons of corporate America, women still don't earn as much as men.

Now, we could celebrate the fact that women are becoming CFOs of such companies as Chevron and Cisco (and we do). These women have climbed to the top. *Brava*. But why aren't the female number crunchers getting paid the same as the men?

I'm sorry; we can't trust the system, Satya. (In his defense, he did quickly backpedal and publicly apologize on Twitter and in a companywide email. His remarks weren't meant to legitimize the wage gap. He's simply gone through his career living by a different set of norms. As Madonna said, "There are rules if you're a girl.") The system has failed us for a few centuries now, and the only thing that's moved the needle are women who misbehave.

## Third Girl's the Charm

Catalyst's 2011 research found that Fortune 500 companies with the most women on the board of directors vs. those with the least have:[3]

- 53 percent higher return on equity
- 42 percent higher return on sales
- 66 percent higher return on invested capital

But here's the kicker: The study found stronger than average results for companies with at least three women serving on the board.

Apparently, third girl's the charm.

Researchers at the Peterson Institute for International Economics in a 2016 study on 21,980 firms across 91 countries that we referenced earlier found no financial benefit from having a woman CEO. However, it did find that going from zero female senior executives to 30 percent led to a 15 percent increase in net revenue. That is, having just one woman at the top did nothing, but having women as almost a third of executives led to an incredible jump in profit . . . which only serves to underscore how critically important it is to unclog the talent pipeline and get women flowing to the top positions.

Here's a paradoxical finding, though: An analysis of 1,500 S&P firms found that, if there was already a woman in one of the top five leadership roles in a company, the chances of hiring another woman executive *fell by 51 percent*—except in companies with a woman CEO. In those instances, the likelihood fell by "only" 30 to 40 percent.[4]

One of my interviewees said, "Gender plays a role if I'm the only woman in the room. If there's another woman, it's less. If there are three, there is no difference. You need critical mass."

Your job is to make sure you're not the only woman in the room. Just talking more doesn't help; you need another woman there to back you up. Not because you're incapable but because you have to communicate strategically.

In 2012, a researcher from Yale studied how U.S. senators' time spent presenting on the Senate floor compared to their relative power and influence.[5] She found that the more male senators talked, the more relative power they possessed. For female senators, however, she found no correlation between how much they spoke and their relative level of power. In a follow-up study, in fact, she found that the more female senators spoke, the more they were ill-perceived by both men *and* women.

Down the street from the Capitol Building, the women in the Obama White House found a way to combat this backlash: Instead of repeating themselves, asserting their points, and trying to ensure they got credit for their own ideas, they began to engage in what they called "amplification." Whenever one woman made a point, another woman in the room would pick up the idea, repeat it, and make sure to point back to the originator of the idea.

> **"The measure of any society is how it treats its women and girls."**
>
> —Michelle Obama

One of my dissertation subjects said, "I've been in a room where I make an articulate statement and everyone shakes their head in disagreement. Then a man will make essentially the same comment and everybody agrees with him. I think to myself, *Didn't I just say that?*"

We're reluctant to say, "Hey! That's my idea!" Like Ms. Chanel Suit on the plane, seeing a man get credit for our work is so common that many of us just shrug and think, *That's OK; it wasn't that big an idea anyway—I'll get the recognition next time. I don't want to make a fuss.*

> **"You can imprison a man, but not an idea.**
> **You can exile a man, but not an idea.**
> **You can kill a man, but not an idea."**
>
> —Benazir Bhutto

To my mind, female White House staffers created a resonance chamber. Instead of a woman combating being interrupted and/or ignored directly, she could rely on a "wing woman" to run interference for her. Not only did this ensure that a woman's voice was explicitly reinforced, but it also helped to combat "bropropriating" (in which a man takes credit for a woman's idea).

But in creating your own alliances, be wary of queen bees.

## Buzzing Queen Bees

A 2015 report found that about twice as many men got help from senior-level men than did their female co-workers. As we discussed in Chapter 1, this is group affinity. It's a unconscious bias, not an explicit one. It's simply a preference for being around "people like us." But what I detest and deplore—with a passion—is the system in place that promotes queen bee behavior.

"Queen bee syndrome" was coined in 1973 to describe highly placed professional women adamantly against any change in traditional gender roles. The poster child for this would probably be Phyllis Schlafly, who successfully fought to keep the Equal Rights Amendment from becoming enshrined in the U.S. Constitution. She was a staunch advocate of a woman's role as a full-time mother and wife, although she herself was an attorney, spoke extensively throughout the U.S., and was a tireless political activist.

(Her most infamous quip: "By getting married, the woman has consented to sex, and I don't think you can call it rape." Talk about a special place in hell . . . )

Over the past four decades, the term queen bee has morphed into describing women in the workplace who are reluctant to help other women and/or hold them to higher standards than they do men.

There are definitely some women who, for whatever reason, do not want to help other women succeed. Maybe they're jealous about sharing the spotlight with another woman. Maybe they're insecure in their own position. Maybe they hate women in general.

I think the real reason lies in cultural constraints. Our society has so few women at the top that we start to believe there is only enough room for one. If you have fought your entire life to make it to the top, and you believe there can be only one woman at those lofty heights because that's what history and the data tell you, then you are going to get all mama-bear. You get so ferocious about protecting your territory that you forget the status quo sucks. It needs to change.

Another scenario I've seen is that senior-level women fear that by helping younger female employees they'll be labeled as "that

# My Queen Bee Experience

After I earned my MBA in London, my husband and I traveled the world, mostly in the South Pacific, for several months before we came back stateside so I could look for a job close to my family. Living near people who know and love you is a blessing, but it can also feel like a curse. I remember them being so fearful: "Did you find a job yet? Do you have any interviews lined up yet? Why hasn't anyone hired you yet?" In retrospect, it only took me a few months to find work, but at the time it felt like an eternity.

Part of the challenge was that I was going after some fairly substantial positions; I didn't want to just take the first thing that came my way.

At one point, I went to an HR recruiter who turned out to be a woman about my age. I went in as my chirpy, happy self, ready to have a pleasant conversation about potentially partnering with her firm to place me in a great position.

She looked at me point-blank and said, "You're a nobody, and you think you can just walk in here and get a job because you went to a fancy school in London?"

I was just stunned. I racked my brain, trying to think how anything I'd said could have been mistaken for that. Inside my head, I was just, like . . . *what?* I mean, I was almost at the end of my rope trying to land a job. I was not assuming that my degree would magically open doors. On the contrary: I was trying to make sure I didn't reek of desperation.

Ladies, we've all encountered women who build themselves up by putting other women down. Maybe they see you as a threat.

Maybe they believe there's only room for one woman in the room, like something out of an old Western: "This town ain't big enough for the two of us!"

How I would navigate that situation now is far different than I did as a new entrant to the work force. How should you deal with these women?

Just as you would if they were a man who was blatantly sexist or racist: Consider their criticisms without taking them personally; don't allow them to determine your self-worth; focus on fulfilling your purpose and making progress toward the team's mission; and smile as you pass them on your way to the top.

woman." The bra-burning women's libber who won't shut up about other women. The woman who should remember that "she only got that job because she's a woman." Fearing this reputation, they temper their advocacy of other women (if they champion them at all). Thank goodness this is changing.

Rear Admiral Grace Hopper spoke at my sister's college graduation. My father, being a military man, was awestruck. Here was the mother of COBOL (I didn't realize how big a deal that was until I got into tech), thrice-retired from the Navy (they kept asking her to come back) who served her country by special congressional approval until her final "retirement" in 1986 at the age of 79 . . . after which she went to work as a senior consultant for an IT company. No wonder her nickname was Amazing Grace. For all her accomplishments, though, she downplayed the significance of her gender. There was a stigma to being a working woman in her generation, and far more so in the military. And, of course, the military certainly didn't want to call attention to it, similar to the unsung contributions of the black women at NASA who enabled John Glenn's historic space flight and inspired the movie *Hidden Figures*: Dorothy Vaughan,

Katherine Johnson, and Mary Jackson. Amazing Grace, like many other amazing women like her, just didn't call attention to the fact that she was female.

Sallie Krawcheck knows how that feels; she used to be one of them.

She began her career as a Wall Street analyst and worked her way up the ranks to become the president of Bank of America's Global Wealth & Investment Management division. She lost her job in 2011 due to a company reorganization. Instead of accepting an offer for another corporate position (and there were plenty), Sallie instead chose to pursue entrepreneurship. She bought a women's networking organization, which she transformed into Ellevate Network, and then founded Ellevest, a platform to help women with financial investments.

She wrote on social media, "For most of my career, I tried to avoid the topic of being a woman in business, vaguely concerned that talking too much about it would hold me back in some way."

Obviously, she's gotten over that . . . but many of her contemporaries haven't. By speaking about gender inequity, the glass ceiling/cliff/elevator, and related issues, they fear it will hurt their chances of rising through the ranks.

I can see their point. There are precious few women at the top (as we've seen again and again). Their executive peers are overwhelmingly male. When it comes time to promote someone, they're afraid that if they back a woman, they'll be accused of bias. Instead of trying to promote a qualified woman, they simply focus on promoting someone qualified . . . and hope that someone else will suggest a woman.

## Be the Rising Tide

*"I wanted to show that women are empowered and strong, and don't necessarily have to be saved by some male hero, but they can take care of themselves using their intelligence and their power."*

—Gal Gadot

Our rebels are different. Like Joan of Arc, they push the limits to not only level the playing field . . . but to hold the door open for bigger and better opportunities.

Supreme Court Justice Ruth Bader Ginsburg told a group of law students that she's often asked how many female justices would be enough, and she always answers, "Nine."

Until Sandra Day O'Connor was appointed in 1981, the court had always had nine men and no one seemed to have a problem with it. Ginsburg wanted to know: Why not nine women?

(It reminds me of when an MSNBC panel debated the wisdom of Hillary Clinton choosing a female running mate. Anita Dunn, former communications director for President Obama, quipped, "Well, there is some precedent for having a running mate of the same gender.")

Our rule breakers want to help as many women as they can rise as high as they can. They don't have a trace of queen bee syndrome. They're not concerned with appearances. They want to back their candidates, throw them in the ring, and "may the best man—or woman—win."

The women I interviewed for my doctoral research were pioneers. When they were coming up through the ranks, there were precious few women they could look to for guidance (if any). They had peers supporting them, but they didn't have anyone at the top backing them.

Now that they're board members, they make it a point to advocate for other women—primarily the ones with whom they've had long-term strategic relationships. In fact, more than a third of them can point to at least one female board member who landed the position with their help.

Often, the more diverse a corporate board is, the more likely it is that they'll promote women to top posts, while all-male boards are more likely to appoint men. One of the most direct ways these women offer peer support is by active nomination. That is, they champion their candidate and advocate to other executives and board members on their behalf. Every great promotion I've landed, every major salary bump I received, and every big job I've secured came about because

# The Weinstein Affair

I am so gratified to see the women who've banded together to come out about being sexually assaulted by Harvey Weinstein, including Angelina Jolie, Gwyneth Paltrow, and Ashley Judd. It took tremendous courage, not only because of the societal shaming that usually follows victims' revelations but because Weinstein's influence could make or break their career. He's one of the most award-winning producers in history and sat on the Oscars board. You don't come out against someone like that lightly.

But almost overnight, the king of Hollywood was knocked off his perch. Once the story broke in *The New York Times* and *The New Yorker*, instead of sitting back in silence, women from all over the industry began adding their stories to the tale and their voices to the outcry.

His wife announced their divorce. The Oscars board voted him off. His political and professional contacts denounced him, including President Obama. Even the board of directors of his own company kicked his ass to the curb.

My heart goes out to all his victims. At the same time, I am heartened to see that we've arrived at a place where even someone as high-profile as Weinstein can be brought to heel for his assault. The issue at the core of sexual harassment, gender inequity, discrimination, and other such topics is really the imbalance of power. There are those who've had it for decades and those who've been at their mercy. That power base is shifting because of women banding together and bringing these injustices to light, supported by those in a place of influence who're finally joining in the conversation.

Hopefully the tale of Harvey Weinstein will serve as both a beacon to those women still suffering in silence and a warning to those who still think they can get away with such abuse.

someone advocated for me when I wasn't in the room. As we discussed in Chapter 8, networking doesn't work; relationship-building does.

Mentor programs don't work because the people assigned to be mentors often don't have the clout to open doors for their mentees. They don't sit in the right rooms, where they could say, "Hey, you know who might be great for that?"

My interviewees were careful to point out, though, that they don't nominate a candidate based on gender. They truly want the best person for the job, regardless of their sex. But because they've networked with like-minded women for so long, they have a long list of qualified people who would be a perfect fit for the job, who happen to be the same gender.

Just like men.

## Move the Needle

Not speaking up certainly hasn't helped close the wage gap. "Trusting the system" hasn't gotten us anywhere. If we want things to change, we have to change them ourselves. In this book, we've focused on how to change things for yourself, but while you do so, consider trying to change things for your fellow women, too.

Why can't you be someone's advocate? Why can't you advance gender equity? Why can't you be the rising tide that lifts others' boats? Why not you? In fact, you may already have more influence than you realize.

A friend of mine worked her way up the ladder until she was the highest-ranking woman in the company. One day, a younger woman approached her and said, "Tina, we need you to do something for all the women here: Wear some pants."

Taken aback, she said, "What? Why?"

"Well, all of us look to you for what we're supposed to do. You always wear dresses and skirts, so we always have, too. If you'd wear some pants, it'd show everyone that it's OK."

Tina had no idea she'd inadvertently set the dress code for women throughout the company. The next day, she came to work in pants. By Monday, there wasn't a skirt to be seen.

If someone like Tina can unwittingly wield such influence, imagine what other behaviors she and her peers might be inadvertently modeling. Do they play favorites? Do they keep quiet in meetings? Do they defer to male colleagues? Do they suffer in silence?

Or do they advocate for gender equity? Do they speak with confidence and advance their ideas? Do they embrace their femininity while demonstrating their competence? Do they tell it like it is?

Whatever you do, you contribute to the culture of your workplace, especially for those behind you who look to you for cues on what's expected of them.

Still, plenty of women worry about being "that woman." They worry they'll be accused of being aggressive, too assertive, or simply a bitch.

**"She was warned. She was given an explanation. Nevertheless, she persisted."**

—Senator Mitch McConnell, on silencing
Senator Elizabeth Warren

You know what? I defy you to find a woman with ambitions beyond the home who *hasn't* been called a bitch. I can't remember a time when I didn't hear that I was "too big for my britches." I've been told I'm too loud, too aggressive, and too ambitious. When I entered the work force, I heard (and still hear) that I'm offensive, too ready to use my platform, too media-hungry, too eager for face time, too attention-grabbing, etc.

I am well-acquainted with what happens when a woman calls attention to herself and, more important, when she points out a deficiency in how society deals with a problem. The fact that I address the issue at all paints a target on my back.

I vividly remember a large tech conference in which I was the moderator for a panel on gender equity and design thinking. I was literally booed—by a crowd of developers! That didn't sting as much as the people who got up and walked out. After checking with the panelists, we came to the conclusion it wasn't the way we presented—it was the content itself. It challenged their long-held beliefs and essentially told them they were wrong. That did not go over well.

This is nothing, of course, compared to what the suffragettes had to go through. I'm not asking for pity. I simply want you to be prepared for what might happen when you use your platform to advance gender equity.

> **"***A man has made at least a start on discovering the meaning of life when he plants shade trees under which he knows full well he will never sit.***"**
>
> —Elton Trueblood

And I had a lot to learn, too. The men who made up 95 percent of the audience needed a more personal approach to begin developing a gender-equity mindset. As we shared findings from the impact of gender on finances and innovation, what the men heard was that they were wrong. When we talked about how technical job descriptions limited the number of women who would apply, the men heard they were wrong and stupid. When we discussed how women in technology are often not heard because they are the only women in the room, they felt blamed and shamed. Follow-up conversations with some of the biggest detractors—who are now some of the best gender-equity advocates I know, by the way— helped me understand how to better present this topic. The men were as much victims of the status quo system as we are, with the same unconscious biases that force us to accept how things are without realizing we are doing so.

*"I want to do it because I want to do it. Women must try to do things as men have tried. When they fail, their failure must be but a challenge to others."*

—Amelia Earhart

While I learned to adapt my messaging for an audience of male influencers, there were still many who just wanted it all to go away. But for every person who's tried to lock this topic in a box hoping it would never see the light of day again, there've been one hundred who cheered the conversation on. It is scary when you first start advocating for a topic like this. It took me years to be comfortable with it. When you use your own platform to advance your cause, you're going to find out quickly who's serious about equity and who's simply paying lip service.

*"Well-behaved women seldom make history."*

—Laurel Thatcher Ulrich

# when women thrive

I thank our lucky stars every day for the work Pat Milligan does. She is shifting mindsets and disrupting industry and the way we lead. By way of introduction: You've heard of the World Economic Forum, aka Davos, right? The place where the who's who of the world come together for a few days a year to try to solve the problems facing the planet?

Pat sits on steering committees for the WEF, is involved in research, and takes the stage as a speaker. She holds the title of global leader for the Multinational Client Group at Mercer. She spearheads Mercer's "When Women Thrive" research. She was also recognized by *Consulting* magazine as one of the top 25 consultants in the United States.

She's kind of a big deal.

*Pat, as a leader in gender equity, you have a unique perspective on where we are in the world.*

On one hand, I am frustrated and disheartened about the real lack of progress we're making on the representation and engagement of women in the global work force. Despite the efforts of people like you, Patti, we're simply not moving the needle.

We've had lots of great conferences, conversations, meetings, surveys, and data, but the fundamental reality is that, as a society, we have not approached equity for women as a real business priority. We need passionate leaders who deeply understand the business and social rationale for having women engaged in the work force—not just women on the board, not women in management, but women working in all levels of the organization. Until we have leaders who understand that, we're missing one of the most important opportunities to advance growth and opportunity in the world—literally.

I feel like there's an edge to this message now: a deep-seated frustration at the lack of real progress and a desire to stop researching this, stop studying this, and get business executives focused on the issue the same way they focus on innovation, sales, and customer satisfaction. That's what it's going to take.

*And yet you say you're optimistic.*

I see examples of great companies with great CEOs and executive teams who are making big commitments and putting passion into this issue the way we've seen other companies make investments and put energy into innovation and risk management. They see that it's an economic imperative that provides real benefits.

You can look across the technology sector, where so many companies are disrupting the idea of what kind of people can succeed in tech. More and more women are moving into software development, sourcing, collaboration, platforms, and communities.

Financial services has seen a lot of progress. That industry experienced severe negative disruption and was threatened to its core. Now, leaders are coming back with an increased focus on risk management and diversified growth. You see Bank of America's vice chairman Anne Finucane calling for greater participation of women in the financial services work force to achieve a more successful, more growth-oriented, less risky company.

The needle is moving in the right direction; it's just doing so slower than we'd like—than we need.

### What moves things in the right direction inside companies?

We see three factors positively correlated with greater gender equity inside a company.

First and foremost, one or more people on the leadership team make work force diversity and inclusion a personal mission. Often, they have a daughter or granddaughter, so gender inclusion becomes more than just a business priority—it's a personal mission. They then communicate that compelling vision to the rest of the executive team, all the way down to middle management. The CEO no longer speaks about gender diversity in broad terms but shares his compelling vision and personal motivations behind the initiative. They begin to invest their own personal time in trying to infuse their vision into the rest of the organization.

Second, they are very specific about how they measure and manage gender diversity and inclusion. They begin to question why the metrics are what they are in different business units.

Third, they realize that this work is not for the weak of heart. They're overcoming an embedded cultural bias that won't disappear overnight. A huge part of the winning formula is that you have to have deep organizational passion and a willingness to disrupt organizational practices that are limiting progress. Leaders have to build the mechanisms that will sustain and continue the work toward gender equity.

*Let's talk about those mechanisms for diversity.*

Before you can know where you're going, you need to know where you are. You have to start with your own work-force analytics and data. What is the shape of your work force? Are you including enough women? Are you promoting them fast enough? What do the data look like for talent acquisition? Retention? Which parts of your work force are irreplaceable?

When executives think about gender diversity, the first thing they often consider are tools and initiatives: "Should we put in a paternity benefit? Do we need to go to flextime?" While those programs may be a piece of the overall process, there are more fundamental considerations.

You need a deep understanding of why women and other diverse populations might want to join your organization. You need to understand not just how diverse your work force is but how inclusive it is. Can your diverse employees bring their full selves to the office? Do they feel they have equal opportunities? Do they believe they'll get promotions based on merit and performance? Do they believe they'll be afforded opportunities for wealth accumulation? Are they staying because they want to or because they have to? Are they leaving in larger numbers than normal turnover would predict?

You have to look at the whole system to understand where you're losing people, where you're not gaining people, and where you're not experiencing full engagement from people.

What I love about your work, Patti, is your passion for using technology to mitigate the biases at every point in an employee's journey through an organization. The more we detect and eliminate those biases, the more we'll see real work-force diversity and inclusion.

Another big success factor we've seen is when companies committed to this issue really involve their men in the middle. When we look at the data globally, we often see the research and attention on women at the top or on the board, but the biggest issue is really the drop-off at the middle-management stage, where women leave at about twice the rate men do.

We've found that male managers, despite being well-intentioned, often aren't equipped to handle women in conversations about stress, flextime, remote working, what the company is willing to do, and other issues that they need to approach differently than they would for their male employees.

When they understand why their female team members are at risk of leaving, and when they're equipped to know how to respond, they can engage their female team members in an incredibly valuable way.

*Let's flip that perspective: What can diversity hires do to move the needle?*

That's a great question. I was running a workshop at the Stanford Business School where 50 percent of the class was women. These are some of the most talented, tech-savvy women of their generation.

I asked how many of them were interviewing or had job offers. I then asked how many would be willing to ask their interviewers any of the following questions: "Do you pay men and women equally for entry-level jobs? Do you promote men and women equally? Do you have a systemic way to measure that there aren't any promotion biases in your organization?"

Their initial reaction was that, no, no one would be willing to do that. But they should. These women are deeply sought after. Companies need them: their talent, their accomplishments, their unique skills—this generation has a powerful advantage the women of my generation didn't have. They should use that to their advantage.

When I work with women's business resource groups, one of my first pieces of advice is "Know your worth." You should know what your economic worth is in the marketplace. You don't have to be aggressive to ask the basic question of how a potential employer will measure that worth and the contributions you provide to their company.

If you're a young woman, your supervisor needs to know that you care about promotion. You care about pay equality. You care about accurate performance reviews. You want to be rewarded equitably for your work.

I'm quite proud of Mercer. We do our own internal labor market analysis, we show the promotion of men and women, we are very clear about why men and women leave, we run focus groups on diversity and inclusion, and we share our pay equity data. Our firm is incredibly transparent. We think holistically, with commitments and focus by our BRGs [business resource groups] on career progression and personal well-being.

***What advice do you give women if they find themselves in companies where they don't feel confident asking those questions or where it seems that gender equity isn't a priority?***

Candidly? If you work in a company that isn't willing to make this a priority, I think you have to ask yourself, "In the long term, am I going to thrive in this environment? Is this where I want to spend the foreseeable future of my professional career?"

Those are tough questions, but they have to be asked.

If I were a young woman entering the job market today, I would want to work for, and I would seek out, those companies that have a serious commitment to diversity and inclusion.

⤜ ⤜ ⤜

*Disrupters* showcases the strategies women in business have used to achieve success. As such, it's focused primarily on what you personally can do. Pat, however, brings up an important point that we haven't discussed much in this book: the necessity of involving men in the process. If we truly want to achieve gender equity, it has to involve all stakeholders.

Pat's pragmatic optimism inspires me, too: When men "get it" and become an ally of feminists, they can become the most powerful champions for women. When they become feminists themselves, they also become evangelists of equitable practices. Once someone in a sociodemographic group sees one of their own doing something, it says two things: This is important enough to do something about, and it's OK for people like us to do this.

I also applaud Pat's suggested first steps: Don't just jump headfirst into some kind of diversity initiative. Gather some intelligence. Look at the data. Define the problem before trying to solve it.

But like the model disrupter she is, Pat also acknowledges the practical side of the situation: Some teams and organizations simply don't want to make diversity and inclusion a priority. It doesn't matter how effective an advocate you are for gender equity; if you're the only proponent of change, you're fighting an uphill battle on a really steep hill. Instead of trying to move the needle by yourself, you might need to seek out another team or employer who's already moving in the right direction.

In other words, if you can't win the game, play somewhere else.

# you're not alone

I had the honor of meeting author Chris Bohjalian at a library in Watertown, Massachusetts. Watertown is the Armenian mecca in our part of the world and the perfect place to hear him do a book reading. I love his books *The Sandcastle Girls* and *Close Your Eyes, Hold Hands* (and really anything he writes). Like me, he is the grandchild of survivors of the Armenian Genocide.

He told us about the last Armenian in Chunkush. He traveled there as part of a group of Armenian-Americans in southern

Turkey, visiting the once-homeland of their forefathers. In one village, they stopped to see a ruined church. This particular village, Chunkush, was the site of a massacre of some 10,000 Armenians. They were rounded up, marched into the desert, and driven off a cliff.

Chris and his friends knew about the massacre, but they also wanted to hear the story from the town's inhabitants. When they'd ask somebody—anybody—about the Armenians who used to live there, the villagers would give vague replies or ignore the question altogether. One person said outright, "We don't talk about that."

As they were getting ready to leave, a man ran up to their van, begging them to come meet his mother-in-law. Chris and company followed the man to his home.

There they met Asiya. It emerged that her mother had been saved from the edge of the cliff at the last moment by one of the soldiers who wanted to marry her (much like my family's story). When Asiya was born, her mother, like many "hidden Armenians," taught her child about their ancestry and heritage.

In her near-century of life, Asiya had never met another Armenian. As Chris' own experience showed, the very subject of Armenians was taboo. Once her mother passed away, Asiya had no one left from the time before.

Chris realized that the man didn't want them to meet Asiya—he wanted Asiya to meet them. His friend translated, as Asiya cried: "I thought I was the only one."

She thought she was the last Armenian in the world.

I want to leave you with that image: a woman who spent a lifetime thinking she was alone. When you fall, when you break, when you feel like there's nothing left of you . . . I want you to know that you're not alone. There are thousands—millions—of us out here just like you. Don't go through life believing you're the only one who struggles with the things you do. Don't believe that your burden is yours to bear alone. Don't believe there's no one out there who understands. Don't believe that your dreams of changing the world or charting your own path aren't worthy. Don't believe that you lack the power, the knowledge, or the strength.

**disrupters**

You're not the only one.

"Ask, and it shall be given you;
seek, and ye shall find;
knock, and it shall be opened unto you."

Welcome to the tribe. We've been waiting for you.

# endnotes

The following are the sources for studies and stats used in this book.

## Chapter 1

[1] "An Analysis of Reasons for the Disparity in Wages Between Men and Women," US Department of Labor; CONSAD Research Corp. (2009).

[2] "Gender Pay Gap Study," Glassdoor (2016). https://www.glassdoor.com/research/app/uploads/sites/2/2016/03/Glassdoor-Gender-Pay-Gap-Study.pdf

[3] "Graduating to a Pay Gap," American Association of University Women (2013). http://www.aauw.org/files/2013/02/graduating-to-a-pay-gap-the-earnings-of-women-and-men-one-year-after-college-graduation.pdf

4 "World Economic Forum Global Gender Gap Report," World Economic Forum (2016). https://www.weforum.org/reports/the-global-gender-gap-report-2016

5 "Studies Show Women and Minority Leaders Have Shorter Tenures, Tenuous Support," Utah State University (2013). http://www.usu.edu/today/index.cfm?id=52537

6 "Women in S&P 500 Companies," Catalyst (2017). http://www.catalyst.org/knowledge/women-sp-500-companies

7 "S&P Global Market Intelligence's Compustat ExecuComp," McGraw-Hill Financial (n.d.). https://marketintelligence.spglobal.com/documents/products/Compustat_ExecuComp_v2.pdf

8 "Women in the Workplace," McKinsey & Co. (2015). http://graphics.wsj.com/women-in-the-workplace/

9 Jacquelyn and Gregory Zehner Foundation.

10 "Venture Capital's Funding Gender Gap Is Actually Getting Worse," *Fortune* (2017). http://fortune.com/2017/03/13/female-founders-venture-capital/

11 "Women in the Boardroom: A Global Perspective, 5th Edition," Deloitte (2017). https://www2.deloitte.com/content/dam/Deloitte/global/Documents/Risk/Women%20in%20the%20boardroom%20a%20global%20perspective%20fifth%20edition.pdf

12 "Why Men Still Get More Promotions Than Women," *Harvard Business Review* (2010). https://hbr.org/2010/09/why-men-still-get-more-promotions-than-women

13 "Examining Exclusion in Woman-Inventor Patenting: A Comparison of Educational Trends and Patent Data in the Era of Computer Engineer Barbie," *Journal of Gender, Social Policy & the Law* (2011).

14 "The Power of Parity: How Advancing Women's Equality Can Add $12 Trillion to Global Growth," McKinsey & Company (2015). https://www.mckinsey.com/global-themes/employment-

and-growth/realizing-gender-equalitys-12-trillion-economic-opportunity

[15] Information in this chart is compiled from the following studies: https://www.nwbc.gov/sites/default/files/FS_Women-Owned_Businesses.pdf https://www.nawbo.org/resources/women-business-owner-statistics http://www.womenable.com/content/userfiles/2016_State_of_Women-Owned_Businesses_Executive_Report.pdf

## Chapter 2

[1] "FAQ About the Armenian Genocide," Armenian National Institute (2017). http://www.armenian-genocide.org/genocidefaq.html

[2] "Workday Planning Gets Worksheets Collaborative Spreadsheets Based on Gridcraft Acquisition," Venture Beat (2016). https://venturebeat.com/2016/09/27/workday-planning-gets-worksheets-collaborative-spreadsheets-based-on-gridcraft-acquisition/

[3] "Gender Bias and Critique of Student Writing," *Assessing Writing*, (1996).

[4] "Women and the Workplace," McKinsey & Co. (2016).

[5] "Women Entrepreneurs 2014: Bridging the Gender Gap in Venture Capital," The Diana Project (2014). http://www.babson.edu/Academics/centers/blank-center/global-research/diana/Documents/diana-project-executive-summary-2014.pdf

[6] "First Round 10-Year Project," First Round (2015). http://10years.firstround.com/

## Chapter 3

[1] "Women in the Workplace 2015," McKinsey & Co. (2015).

[2] "Black Women: Ready to Lead," Center for Talent Innovation (2015). http://www.talentinnovation.org/publication.cfm?publication=1460

3 "The Sandwich Generation," Pew Research Center (2013).

4 "Why Women Are Leaving Corporate America in Droves," Escape from Corporate America Blog (2004). http://www. escapefromcorporateamerica.com/2004/08/why-women-are-leaving-corporate.html?m=1

5 "Women in the Workplace," McKinsey & Co (2017). https:// womenintheworkplace.com/Women_in_the_Workplace_2017.pdf

6 "The Lived Experiences of Women in Executive Positions of the U.S. Federal Civil Service, " C.B. Williams (2005).

7 "Women Matter," McKinsey & Company (2012).

8 "Analysis of Telecommuting Statistics from 2005-2015," U.S. Census Bureau American Community Survey (2016). http:// globalworkplaceanalytics.com/telecommuting-statistics

9 "Breadwinner Moms," Pew Research Center (2013). http://www. pewsocialtrends.org/2013/05/29/breadwinner-moms/

10 "Who's Breadwinning in Europe? A Comparative Analysis Of Materal Breadwinning in Great Britain and Germany," The Progressive Policy Think Tank (2015). https://www.ippr.org/ publications/whos-breadwinning-in-europe

11 "Uncovering Talent: A New Model of Inclusion," Deloitte (2013). https://www2.deloitte.com/content/dam/Deloitte/us/Documents/ about-deloitte/us-inclusion-uncovering-talent.pdf

## Chapter 4

1 "The Rise in Dual Income Households," Pew Research Center (2015). http://www.pewresearch.org/ft_dual-income-households-1960-2012-2/

2 2010 U.S. Census. https://www.census.gov/2010census/

3 "Who's Breadwinning in Europe?" Institute for Public Policy Research (2015). https://www.ippr.org/publications/whos-breadwinning-in-europe

4 U.S. Census Bureau 2011 American Community Survey. https://www.census.gov/programs-surveys/acs

5 "Who's Breadwinning in Europe?" Institute for Public Policy Research (2015). https://www.ippr.org/publications/whos-breadwinning-in-europe

6 "Breadwinner Moms," Pew Research Center (2013). http://www.pewsocialtrends.org/2013/05/29/breadwinner-moms/

## Chapter 5

1 "Women in the Workplace," McKinsey & Co. (2016).

2 "Voice Pitch and the Labor Market Success of Male Chief Executive Officers," *Evolution and Human Behavior* (2013).

3 "Demographics of Key Social Networking Platforms," Pew Research Center (2014). http://www.pewinternet.org/2015/01/09/demographics-of-key-social-networking-platforms-2/

4 "The Glass Cliff: Evidence that Women Are Over-Represented in Precarious Leadership Positions," *British Journal of Management* (2005). http://onlinelibrary.wiley.com/doi/10.1111/j.1467-8551.2005.00433.x/abstract;jsessionid=8F808F56194C780C6E5C906AC806456E.f03t01

5 "Above the Glass Ceiling: When Are Women and Racial/Ethnic Minorities Promoted to CEO?" *Strategic Management Journal* (2013).

6 "Reactions to the Glass Cliff: Gender Differences in the Explanations for the Precariousness of Women's Leadership Positions," *Journal of Organizational Change Management* (2007).

7 "2013 Chief Executive Study: Women CEOs of the Last 10 Years," Strategy & (2014). https://www.strategyand.pwc.com/reports/2013-chief-executive-study

8 "Above the Glass Ceiling: When Are Women and Racial/Ethnic Minorities Promoted to CEO?" *Strategic Management Journal* (2013).

9 "The Glass Cliff: When and Why Women Are Selected as Leaders in Crisis Contexts," *British Journal of Social Psychology* (2010).

10 "Moving Women to the Top: McKinsey Global Survey Results," McKinsey & Co. (2010).

11 "The CS Gender 3000: Women in Senior Management," Credit Suisse (2014); "Diversity Matters," McKinsey & Co. (2015). https://publications.credit-suisse.com/tasks/render/file/index. cfm?fileid=8128F3C0-99BC-22E6-838E2A5B1E4366DF

12 "Women in Alternative Investments Report," KPMG (2016); "Women in Alternative Investments: A Marathon, Not a Sprint," Rothstein Kass, (2014). https://www.managedfunds.org/industry-resources/industry-research/women-alternative-investments-marathon-sprint-rothstein-kass/

13 "Why Diversity Matters," Catalyst Information Center (2013). http://www.catalyst.org/system/files/why_diversity_matters_catalyst_0.pdf

14 "How Gender Bias Corrupts Performance Reviews, and What to Do About It," *Harvard Business Review* (2017). https://hbr.org/2017/04/how-gender-bias-corrupts-performance-reviews-and-what-to-do-about-it. "Research: Vague Feedback Is Holding Women Back," *Harvard Business Review* (2016). https://hbr.org/2016/04/research-vague-feedback-is-holding-women-back

## Chapter 6

1 "Investigating the World's Rich and Powerful: Education, Cognitive Ability, and Sex Differences," *Intelligence* (2014). https://www.psychologytoday.com/files/attachments/56143/wai-the-global-elite-in-press.pdf

2 "Top 9 Companies for Executive Women," Diversity Inc. (2016). http://www.diversityinc.com/top-companies-executive-women/

3 "Salary Difference Between Male and Female Registered Nurses in the United States," *Journal of the American Medical Association* (2015). https://jamanetwork.com/journals/jama/fullarticle/2208795

[4] "Professors in the Boardroom and Their Impact on Corporate Governance and Firm Performance," *Financial Management* (2015). http://onlinelibrary.wiley.com/doi/10.1111/fima.12069/abstract

[5] "Do Gay-Friendly Corporate Policies Enhance Firm Performance?" *SSRN Electronic Journal* (2013).

[6] "Multicultural Women at Work," *Working Mother* (2015). http://www.workingmother.com/tags/multicultural-women

[7] "Are You Ready to Manage Five Generations of Workers?" *Harvard Business Review* (2009). https://hbr.org/2009/10/are-you-ready-to-manage-five-g

[8] "Top Management Team Nationality Diversity and Firm Performance: A Multilevel Study," *Strategic Management Journal* (2012).

## Chapter 7

[1] "Why Diversity Programs Fail," *Harvard Business Review* (2016). https://hbr.org/2016/07/why-diversity-programs-fail

[2] "Women as Mentors: Does She or Doesn't She?" DDI (2013). http://www.ddiworld.com/ddi/media/trend-research/womenasmentors_rr_ddi.pdf?ext=.pdf

[3] "Delusions of Progress," *Women in Management* (2010). https://hbr.org/2010/03/women-in-management-delusions-of-progress

## Chapter 8

[1] The Diana Project 1999. www.dianaproject.org

[2] "Women Entrepreneurs 2014: Bridging the Gender Gap in Venture Capital," The Diana Project (2014).

[3] "First Round 10-Year Project," First Round (2015). http://10years.firstround.com/

[4] "Playing the Boys' Game: Golf Buddies and Board Diversity," *American Economic Review* (2016).

5 "Male Allies: Men Convince Other Men That Gender Equity Matters," Society of Industrial-Organizational Psychologists Conference (2016).

## Chapter 10

1 "Microsoft CEO Satya Nadella to Women: Don't Ask for Raise, Trust Karma," Readwrite (2014). https://readwrite.com/2014/10/09/nadella-women-dont-ask-for-raise/

2 "Female CFOs Underpaid by 16% on Average," GMI Ratings Boardroom Diversity Project (2013). http://www.boardroomdiversity.org/tag/gmi/

3 "The Bottom Line: Corporate Performance and Women's Representations on Boards," Catalyst 2007. http://www.catalyst.org/knowledge/bottom-line-corporate-performance-and-womens-representation-boards

4 "Is There an Implicit Quota in Women in Top Management? A Large-Sample Statistical Analysis," *Strategic Management Journal* (2016).

5 "Who Take the Floor and Why: Gender, Power, and Volubility in Organizations," *Administrative Science Quarterly* (2012).

# resources

There are thousands of worthy organizations that engage women, create community, and build strong relationships. I can't list them all, but below are a few of my favorites. Share yours with me on Twitter at @pkfletcher or Facebook at http://facebook. com/drpattifletcher.

## Start Local!

Local organizations are a great place to start. Heather Boggini belongs to Working Women of Tampa Bay (workingwomenoftampabay. com/), and I participate with MetroWest Conference for Women (www.metrowestconferenceforwomen.org/). If you can't find anything in your neck of the woods, why not start your own tribe?

## Organizations and Research

**Anita Borg Institute**

https://anitaborg.org/

Women in technology are at the heart of ABI's mission. ABI is on a quest to accelerate the pace of global innovation by working to ensure that the creators of technology mirror the people and societies that use it.

**Astia**

http://astia.org/

Astia is a community of experts committed to leveling the playing field for women entrepreneurs by providing access to capital and networks for the companies they lead.

**Babson WIN Lab**

http://www.babson.edu/Academics/centers/cwel/educational-programs/win-lab/Pages/home.aspx

Babson College's Women Innovating Now (WIN) Lab is an eight-month residency program for women entrepreneurs who are ready to think big, be bold, and launch successful companies.

**The Diana Project**

www.babson.edu/Academics/centers/blank-center/global-research/diana/Pages/home.aspx

The Diana Project engages in research activities, forums, and scholarship focusing on women entrepreneurs and their growth.

**McKinsey's "Women in the Workplace 2017" Study**

https://womenintheworkplace.com/

This is a comprehensive study on the state of women in corporate America. The study is part of a long-term partnership between LeanIn.Org and McKinsey & Company to give companies the information they need to promote female leadership and foster gender equality in the workplace.

**When Women Thrive**

www.mercer.com/our-thinking/when-women-thrive.html

When Women Thrive is Mercer's global research and solution platform designed to help organizations drive growth through the active and productive participation of their female work force.

## Conferences and Events

### ChIPs

http://chipsnetwork.org/

ChIPs is a 501(c)(3) corporation with more than 1,500 members dedicated to advancing women at the confluence of technology, law, and policy. It serves the dual purpose of increasing diversity and inclusion in these fields, as well as accelerating the progress of innovation that benefits our society.

### Emerging Women Live

http://emergingwomenlive.com

The conference of the broader organization Emerging Women, a global network encouraging feminine leadership and entrepreneurship for all women in all sectors at all levels.

### Grace Hopper Celebration of Women in Computing

https://ghc.anitaborg.org/

The Grace Hopper Celebration of Women in Computing is the world's largest gathering of women technologists. It is produced by the Anita Borg Institute and presented in partnership with the Association for Computing Machinery.

### The Massachusetts Conference for Women

www.maconferenceforwomen.org/

The Massachusetts Conference for Women provides connection, motivation, networking, inspiration, and skill building for thousands of women each year.

### S.H.E. Summit

https://shesummit.com/

The S.H.E. Summit is the renowned yearly global leadership conference that celebrates and accelerates the advancement of women and gender equality.

## Online Communities and Resources

**DailyWorth**
www.dailyworth.com/

**DiversityInc**
www.diversityinc.com/

**Ellevate Network**
www.ellevatenetwork.com/

**Ellevest**
www.ellevest.com/

**Girls Who Code**
girlswhocode.com/

**Women Entrepreneur**
www.facebook.com/womenent/

**Working Mother**
www.workingmother.com/

**WorthFM**
www.worthfm.com/

## Books to Read

These are some of my favorite books about women, disruption, and the world. Check them out:

*#GirlBoss*, Sophia Amoruso

*A Higher Standard: Leadership Strategies from America's First Female Four-Star General*, Ann Dunwoody

*A New Earth: Awakening to Your Life's Purpose*, Eckhart Tolle

*Bossypants*, Tina Fey

*By Invitation Only: How We Built Gilt and Changed the Way Millions Shop*, Alexis Maybank and Alexandra Wilkis Wilson

*Close Your Eyes, Hold Hands*, Chris Bohjalian

*Daring Greatly: How the Courage to Be Vulnerable Transforms the Way We Live, Love, Parent, and Lead*, Brené Brown

*Drop the Ball: Achieving More by Doing Less*, Tiffany Dufu

*Earning It: Hard-Won Lessons from Trailblazing Women at the Top of the Business World*, Joann S. Lublin

*Girl Code: Unlocking the Secrets to Success, Sanity, and Happiness for the Female Entrepreneur*, Cara Alwill Leyba

*How Remarkable Women Lead: The Breakthrough Model for Work and Life*, Joanna Barsh, Susie Cranston, and Geoffrey Lewis

*In the Company of Women: Inspiration and Advice from Over 100 Makers, Artists, and Entrepreneurs*, Grace Bonney

*Lean In: Women, Work, and the Will to Lead*, Sheryl Sandberg

*Nice Girls Don't Get the Corner Office: Unconscious Mistakes Women Make That Sabotage Their Careers*, Lois P. Frankel

*Originals: How Non-Conformists Move the World*, Adam Grant

*Own It: The Power of Women at Work*, Sallie Krawcheck

*Presence: Bringing Your Boldest Self to Your Biggest Challenges*, Amy Cuddy

*So Good They Can't Ignore You: Why Skills Trump Passion in the Quest for Work You Love*, Cal Newport

*Stiletto Network: Inside the Women's Power Circles That Are Changing the Face of Business*, Pamela Ryckman

*Thrive: The Third Metric to Redefining Success and Creating a Life of Well-Being, Wisdom, and Wonder*, Arianna Huffington

*What I Told My Daughter: Lessons from Leaders on Raising the Next Generation of Empowered Women*, Nina Tassler

*Worth It: Your Life, Your Money, Your Terms*, Amanda Steinberg

# acknowledgments

To say I am rich with love is an understatement. No one gets to the finish line alone. I am honored and grateful for the many people who have helped make this book happen: a ten-year journey filled with laughter, awakening, and love. Thank you.

*Heather Boggini*: I am so happy I don't have to find out what being a disrupter would be like without a best friend and business partner with me every step of the way. I am humbled beyond words by everything you do to partner with me on enabling leaders to change the world for the better.

*Chris, Gabby, Bella, and Winnie Fletcher*: I am grateful for your love, patience, caring, and understanding of the craziness I always bring to our home. Without you, I would be paralyzed. You are my foundation—the source of the strength I need to go out and fight another day.

*Derek Lewis*: I truly could not have done this without you. I am so, so grateful for your time, thoughtfulness, and dedication to creating a book I am proud to share with my fellow disrupters.

*Vanessa Campos, Jennifer Dorsey, Danielle Brown, and Ralph Li at Entrepreneur Media*: Thank you for taking a risk on this book. Your vision, enthusiasm, and support have made everything about this adventure a dream come true.

*My dissertation participants*: It's been almost ten years, and I am still learning from you and sharing your wisdom. You taught me the importance of building a platform and using it to change the world for the better. Thank you for changing my life.

*Gabby Burlacu, Miriam Christof, Anula Jayasuriya, Jo-Ann Mendles, Pat Milligan, Lisa Morales-Hellebo, Tanya Odom, Brenda Reid, Nicole Sahin, and Surbhi Sarna*: I am honored that you trusted me to share your story. I am in awe of you, the disruption you've endured, and the disruption you have led.

*Kim Gruenberg*: You have taught me what it means to lead gracefully; to enable everyone, even the most vulnerable and at-risk; and to use disruption as the starting point for good.

*My coaching clients*: I can't name you, but I must acknowledge you. Every day, you lead through change . . . and invite me to come along with you. Seeing you transform is awe-inspiring. You are my daily source of inspiration and, knowing how much good is out there in the world, comfort. You *are* the disrupters this book is for.

*Astia, Astia Angels, The Boston Club, my fellow Boston tribe members, Geraldine Lim, Ashley Colombo, Dorit Shackleton, Stephanie Buscemi, Katie Forsythe, and Jonathan Becher*: Thank you for nonstop support and motivation as you continue to lead the way and break the mold.

*Marcia Soares, Sheri Rhodine, and Jenean Fields-Hansen*: Thank you for enabling some of the world's most amazing leaders—for disrupting the bad and replacing it with good. You are the disrupters I look up to, and I am honored to call you colleagues and, more important, friends.

# Index